THOUGHTS OF DISCORD

DOMINIC LYNE

I0104910

Published by **Degraded Discord**
an imprint of **DPL Publishing**, 2012

www.dom-lyne.co.uk

ISBN: 978-0-9561612-2-2

For all those that have stuck by me.
You know who you are.

THOUGHTS OF DISCORD

DOMINIC LYNE

BOOK ONE
SELF DEGRADED SUICIDE

$C_{16}H_{13}CIN_2O$

23 September 2006

What to write? What to say? How simple thoughts sound in your head, how hard to word. Go back a year. Fucked off my face. Existing in an alternate world. Chemically calm or chemically enhanced? The choice always a pill, a line, a glass. Record the pain; get it out from the head. Let the words echo into the air, vibrations locked in the surroundings for eternity. My soul bled, my arms drummed, my voice sang.

Then it stopped. Waking up one day with no memories, no plastic in your wallet, and no one around does that to you. A turning point. Time to get off, clean up, focus. December 31, record the most painful memories to tape. As the last word leaves the lips, the clocks chime. Happy New Year.

In your absence the knives are sharpened. Conversations behind your back, the rot sets in. When you're not a part of it, you can see things clearly. Then the knife is pushed. Pushed so far into your back. It cuts deep, one of the deepest amongst those other scars. When you've been stabbed so many times in the back by the people you held dearest, you know what to do. Pull it out and let the blood flow. Cut the anger to music. A new vitriol for the voice. Stand up and move on. Dead.

Finished. With nothing to do you realise what you've been doing. Find as many ways to block things from your mind. Chemicals or music, either way you think about nothing but that. Then when there's nothing it floods back. The emptiness. Half your soul missing and no one cares. People too consumed with themselves to actually give a shit about you.

Hand on the mirror, the shadow standing in the corner.

Always the corner. Waiting. Inside your head you are slowly rotting. Your eyes are open and you see the tears running down your face. You feel nothing, empty. Life rolling on day by day. Sleep, wake, exist. No one gives a shit about anyone but themselves.

So you sit and write. Memories and emotions poured out like ink spills across a page. Maybe this will help; maybe it will deepen the emptiness. Once your soul mourns it will never stop. You know that. Too many people interfere and everything is lost forever.

I wish there was a switch, something that would just turn it off. But there's nothing, no way to feel nothing. Mother, please tell me why. Tell me why it sticks in my head. Tell me why it hurts so much. Tell me why I can't just close my eyes. Please tell me why it won't all just fade away.

How can you smile with a gun to my head?

Locked in limbo, Purgatory or Hell? It's a matter of hope. Chemicals controlling your reactions, emotions controlling the chemicals. Let nature take control or opt for synthetic feelings. It's a matter of choice.

Each day I kill two hundred and twenty minutes of my future. A slow suicide. Destroying cells, burning the insides. Cancer. Man made or mankind? Kill the body that created you. Dirt, death, decay. How easy all of those set in.

One chance, one redemption, one way of escape. Everything only happens once. Hope is changeable, fate eternal.

In our heads we create a world. Thousands of lives and we choose our own cast. Our world's populace aimed at making us comfortable, aimed at challenging us, aimed at making us happy. Our world remains the same, only the population changes. The question we need to ask, do we create worlds or prisons? Locked up and governed over. If they are prisons, then who holds the keys? Can we ever be free? Will we only find release on death? Our lives a punishment; living on death row awaiting the end.

If I click my fingers hard enough will I awake in another world? A padded cell or a coma patient? The world around me bends, distorts, glimmers of another just around the corner. Rip, tear, wake. If I'm sleeping is this a dream or a nightmare? Living in Hell, a flaming pitchfork pressed against my back. A brand, a scar, a torture.

Almost two years ago a stranger with a black eye gave two people on a train some advice. He said to take care of each other, be there for each other. A stranger saw what those two had and selflessly gave his advice. He had nothing to gain and nothing to lose. A stranger saw what was felt and told the two to make sure they never lost sight of that. I listened. I understood.

This is my way of understanding, my way of closing a period of my life. This is an explanation, a testimonial, a breakdown and redemption. This is the hardcopy of a moment of time burnt to disc.

Apologies for any inconvenience caused.

this is where we come in

It always feels like your first Alcoholic's Anonymous meeting when you let someone into your life. Trying to find a suitable way to introduce yourself. Coming to terms with the idea that this is the start of a journey. So where to begin? So many possibilities, but the logical point would be to start here. I'll spare you the long, drawn out explanation of who I am, where I've come from and what I'm like. I won't fill your heads with images of how I want you to see me, I'll let you form your own opinions based on what you read. Think what you want and I'll do exactly the same.

So anyway, here I am, sat on a train, heading in one direction with no turning back. Without needing to see them I know my eyes are going to be bloodshot and watery, crying has that effect on them. That's right; I've been crying in public, none of that 'save your tears for when no one's looking' crap here. Show your emotions openly, that way you'll look like you're alive, not just an automated mannequin.

What an interesting point to begin at. The start of this is an end to a part of my life. Well, technically it's already ended and this is the aftermath. So, why the tears? Why the train? Why the empty feeling deep inside of me? I've just had my heart ripped out and stamped on by the centre of my world, or in plain and simple English, I've just broken up with someone I loved above all else. I won't go into the reasons as it hurts too much, it still hasn't sunken in, my mind fresh with my Hollywood style ending. The unhappy ending. The 'frankly my dear, I don't give a damn' exit. No looking over the shoulder, a forward walk in one direction. Home. Guildford.

If I'm perfectly honest, my mind's numb. Cold,

unthinking. Unthinking by choice. I don't want to run everything through my head. I want to hold onto the fading notion of hope that this will all blow over, that within days we'll be sat laughing about it. A glimmer of hope shining in the night sky. Deep down I know that the star will soon fade and then it'll wash over me, until that day I guess it's just carry on as normal. I'm crap with break ups.

So here I am, on a train, hurtling through the country towards a destination. Counting down the station stops in my head, I've travelled this route so many times I know them by heart. The train slows to a stop. Cobham and Stoke D'Abernon.

Look outside the window, the blurred scenery could be anywhere, no landmarks to distinguish it to memory. Thoughts, memories replaying before daydreamed eyes. Zoned out in your own world; iPod streaming digitised music into your head. Your own personal soundtrack, create play-lists to fit your mood. It's hard to say what I'm thinking, hard for one obvious reason. Consciously I'm not thinking anything, just letting the moment take hold. I have a knack of doing that. If I don't want to think, I focus on nothing in the distance, let the eye's vision blur and let the mind empty. No thoughts, no worries. How peaceful it must be to be a zombie, living in a dreamless, waking sleep.

I've been on trains all day. The uncomfortable journey back from Preston to Euston, three and a half hours contemplating the fast approaching end, each thought another second closer, inescapable, a journey towards a knowing death. Having picked up my things from their house, it's the return to the Underground, a place of memories, walking through the barriers at Highbury and Islington knowing it'll be for the last time for the foreseeable future, no need to grace the station with my regular presence. Victoria line, change at Euston for the Northern line to Waterloo. The journey home, alone, the long train, free if you avoid the ticket inspectors.

The train slows. Focus. Clandon. I've missed a few, the

next station the one at which I make my exit from this train. Open my bag. Pull out my tobacco, filters and papers. My favourites: Golden Virginia and Rizla blues. Roll, lick, seal. Smile to myself as I zip up the bag and get ready. His grandparents brought me about five packets of tobacco back from their holiday; it should see me through for a while. Rise and move to the door. Click, flame, inhale. It's a non-smoking carriage but it's empty so who's here to complain?

You've joined me at a weird point in my life. It's the start of a new chapter, a new journey. New adventures to be had. The train begins to slow. London Road, Guildford.

The only way is down.

the wrong end of the law

I'm running, a fast paced movement. I don't quite fancy walking down an unknown, unlit alley at this time of night, or rather morning. I mean it's not fear that compels me to run but the fact that three hours ago I said I was going for a breath of fresh air and I don't want to bump into anything that would further delay my return journey. Out of the alley and across the road.

Noise, dogs barking. The late night slap of my feet against the solid floor must have woken them, disturbing quiet sleep with frantic barks. Ignore and move on, what harm can a few dog howls do to me? I've only moved a few paces before I hear it, the familiar pad of feet, human and animal chasing after me, a shout, human. A shout commanding me to stop. Well, I don't know about you but when I hear someone shouting as they dash after me in the middle of the night, I'm not likely to stop running. My feet continue.

'Stop! Police.'

Okay, that changes everything.

My feet come to a dramatic stop, emergency brake. Four men approaching, two holding a dog; a barking dog eager to grip me by the arm if given the chance. Smile Dom, keep smiling, not that that's hard anyway.

'Can you tell me what you're doing?' One asks, I guess he's gonna be the bad cop.

'Walking home.'

'At this time? Where've you come from?'

'My mates.' A lie, small but necessary.

'Well we've just had a report of criminal damage and what do we find? You running out of the scene of crime.'

'Really? Like I said I've been with a mate.'

'You understand how this looks?'

'Maybe.'

'Can you tell me what you were doing with your 'mate'?'

Now you see, that's the problem. This is where I'm stuck for words, I mean I can't just turn around and say 'Fucking, and besides he's not my mate we only just met for sex.' Well I could but they look pissed off with me already. I settle for 'Talking.'

'Talking? Talking all night?'

'Well I didn't think that was a crime.'

Bad cop takes a step closer. 'Less of the attitude.' He nods to the other cop, obviously the good cop. A proper cop, dressed in uniform, bad cop just in his suit. 'Search him,' says bad cop.

I watch good cop pull out a pair of purple gloves and put them on. He's hot, cute, good looking and short brown hair. He smiles at me as he begins to frisk me down. I can't help but get a boner. His hand touches it as he searches my front pocket. He looks up at me, smirk on his face. I smile back, I bet you he's blushing. The search continues and finishes with a search of my coat pocket. He pulls out its content. A near empty pouch of tobacco and king-sized Rizlas. I had totally forgotten about those. Good cop hands them to bad cop.

'What are these?' demands bad cop.

'Tobacco and Rizla,' I reply.

'What are they doing in your pocket?'

'I smoke obviously. I know dirty habit but hardly illegal.' I'm smiling like the Cheshire Cat.

Bad cop snarls. 'King-sized papers?'

'Well you know, you ask for blue and they just assume that's what you want.'

'Right.' He doesn't believe me, I can tell. My hands are too fidgety, my mood too hyper. 'Have you been taking drugs tonight sir?'

'Me?' I laugh. 'Never.'

'Have you been selling drugs?'

'Not that I know of.'

'I'll ask you again. Have you taken drugs this evening?'

'Such a long time, I'm not sure. Nah, not that I remember. You can do a test if you want.' Fuck why did I say that?

'It won't be necessary. So what was your friend's name and house number?'

I tell them the address but I stumble for the name. I remember him saying it but it wasn't important enough to remember. It began with a T. I'm sure it did. 'Tim,' I offer.

Bad cop walks away, using his phone to perform a name check, fucking bastard. He returns. 'The person at that address is called Anthony.'

I smile sweetly. 'Tony, Timothy. Same thing really. I'm crap with names.'

Bad cop shakes his head. 'We're getting nowhere. We'll let you off with a warning. Are you known to the police?'

'I dunno, do you know of me?'

Bad cop snarls and turns to good cop. 'Finish up here.' He walks away leaving good cop to give me a yellow piece of paper informing me that I've been up to no good so was stopped and searched.

'Keep out of mischief,' he says with a smile as I turn to leave.

'I'll try, no promises.' I laugh and bounce off like Tigger. I know they're following but I don't care. It's almost three in the morning and I'm fucking knackered.

A week passes with a causal monotony, then I'm in the kitchen one day and my landlady asks if I've finished. I say I have, stir my cup of tea and begin to leave. As I walk out there's two coppers standing there. Heart stops for a second, then I walk past saying 'hello' to one of them. The one who was giving me the weird look. The same copper who performed the search on me with his purple gloves. The same copper who came up to my room to ask me for my number.

Two days later, a Saturday and I get a phone call. It's good cop, he's in the area and wants to meet up. 'Okay,' I say and that's why here I am, handcuffed to the headboard getting sucked off by a policeman. It's a shame his beauty doesn't extend all over. Not that I'm a size queen but his dick has to be the smallest I've ever seen. No word of a lie it's the size of my thumb. How do you do anything with that? He wants me to fuck him, so I guess in my current state that means he's gonna be on top. Can't complain though, he's cute.

He still thinks I'm a druggie, but at least, for once, it's the lawbreaker fucking the law over and not losing. I want to laugh but he might take offence. I guess it's all in the line of duty.

$C_{23}H_{28}O_8$

Mama told me to be careful in the people that I chose,
But I never stopped to notice as I went about this life.
Now I sit here and I wonder were they friends or just foes?
All those guys were a commodity; lost the only one I loved.
Papa never say a word no, about anything I've done.
Counting numbers in my head now, after thirty you feel numb.
Sickened by my own admission, tired lies are wearing thin.
For all those people that have hurt me, lost the only one I
    loved.
Brother's always there to help me.
The past has nothing left to say,
But I never stopped to notice as I lost the only one I loved.
But what if they were all illusions?
Silent ghosts from long ago.
What if they could all remember?
Could they picture me at all?

a false start

It's late September and everything is ready. Guide tracks written and prepared, an initial track-listing worked out. So this is it. The start of a project without title. Welcome to the entrance, there's no turning back now.

For once I have direction, a meaning. A goal that must be achieved no matter what. The end date is set in stone, there's no avoiding that. I'm not used to working to deadlines so this is going to be somewhat interesting. So let's get this show on the road. I pull my bag onto my shoulders and leave the house. I'm smiling; everything feels good. So this is what it feels like to be following the path of destiny.

Judas is stood waiting for me as I arrive; we're both early as we had agreed. Time to sort ourselves out and talk about what we aim to achieve from this first session.

We settle down at a table in the pub, a corner table so we can talk in peace, two pints of coke keep our throats moist. You know the rules, no drink, no drugs before a recording session. You need to keep the mind sharp. This means so much to me that nothing must ruin it. Judas understands this, that's why he's offered to help even though we're months away from laying down the first tracks of guitars. He'll be my tape operator. Pressing record for me as I perform in the live room.

The hands on the clock move round faster than we anticipate, pick up our things and leave. Just enough time for one more cigarette. Roll. Click, flame, inhale. There's no nerves running through me, no feelings of apprehension. I've been in the studio too many times for that. It's work; well the performance and production side is anyway. Yet something feels different, this time it feels right, like I'm meant to be doing this recording, that it will actually make a change to my own personal outlook on life. I've been preparing for a year for this moment, and now it arrives. Without fanfare or parade.

'You're very quiet,' Judas says.

I look at him, my eyes focusing out of a daydream. 'Just getting my mind in the zone.' I smile, stub my cigarette out on the wall and let its crushed corpse fall to the ground. 'Let's go do this.'

Type in the door code; walk up the flights of steps, collecting the box of microphones on our way. I've decided we're starting from the ground up. Today I'll be drumming for five hours.

The problem when talking about studio sessions is that they sound boring, you have to set up, plug in and re-adjust all the mics, inputs and change damaged leads. There's not many ways you can write about that in an interesting word flow. Oh, I plugged the XLR into channel 13 and then routed the backing tracks to another channel. Like any job you enjoy, it's mundane to talk about, yet it gives so much satisfaction to you because of the ease at which you do it. An accountant has his numbers; I have my patch leads and faders. So I'll spare you all of the details and processes.

I smile; it's only taken us half an hour to sort everything out. From the control room I look through the glass and watch Judas as he just makes some final alterations around the drum kit. When he's done we'll go out for a cigarette, I know once I start drumming I won't take a break until the tasks are done. One cigarette, then the record button will be pushed for the first time on this project. Then it will have truly begun.

We return to the studio, our lungs burning, our minds focused on what we are about to achieve. I pick up my drumsticks.

'Time for the sound check dude,' Judas says. He smiles. 'Go beat the shit out of those drums.'

I laugh. 'I fucking intend to.'

Enter the live room, sit down and play. Through the

window I can see Judas altering the inputs. Keep everything out of the red. He stops and moves over to my bag, when he returns he's holding up my phone. I hear his voice through talkback. 'Your phone dude, it's called twice.'

I nod and get up, as I walk to the control room Judas appears, holding a silent phone. 'I need to adjust something, but other than that it's sounding sweet.'

'Cool,' I say as I take the phone. It rings as though sensing my touch. My eyes flick to the caller ID. My heart sinks, what does he want? 'I won't be long.'

Turn the corner and flip open the phone. 'Yeah?' I say into the receiver.

'Hey Dom, it's Sam.'

I knew that much already. My pause lasts a beat too long.

'Dom?'

'Sorry, was sidetracked.' I really don't need this right now. 'What's up?'

'Just wanted to check that you're alright.'

'Yeah I'm fine. My usual self. Keeping busy, you know how it is.' Well if he did, he knew more than me.

'Ahh cool, what you up to?' I hear his Nan's voice in the background. It could almost be like the old days.

'I'm in the studio at the moment, so kinda busy.'

'Oh, sorry. I'll let you get on with it.'

'No, it's cool.' The reply rushing from my mouth a bit too quickly. Compose yourself. Speak. 'Okay then. Hope you're well.'

'Yeah I'm good, just off out in a minute, was just phoning to see if you were okay.'

'Cool. Bye then.'

A pause. 'Yeah, bye.'

I let my ear listen to the silence of background noise coming from his end. Will he speak again? Will he hang up?

I snap the phone shut, cutting off the connection. My concentration in the recording gone. The barriers knocked I can feel the emptiness at my core. I can sense its growth, spreading like a cancer hidden until it's too late. Why the fuck did he have to phone? Why the fuck did he have to enter back into my life for those stumbled few minutes?

I look up and see Judas turn and give me the thumbs up. I point to the headphones. He puts them on. 'Dude,' I say with my finger on the talkback button. 'I'm just going to the toilet.'

He nods, picks up my sticks and attempts to play a left handed drum kit.

My phone rings as I leave the room. Flip it open. 'Yep.'

'So everything's okay with you?' Sam's voice.

'Everything is fine.' My voice sharp.

'Okay, I just needed to know.' In that moment I know he actually meant those words.

'Bye Sam.' I snap the phone closed without waiting for a reply. I dunno why. I push open the door to the toilet and stand in front of the mirror.

I can see the tears in my eyes, glazing the eyeballs. I will not cry. You can fuck off if you think I'm going to cry. Do you really think *he* is feeling this? He's got his friends to help him through; you've got your music. Breathe and get on with it.

I sigh, rub my hands down my face. I would switch my phone off but I know it's not going to ring. That number will never call mine again. In silence I feel a shadow pass over me. It's here, it's waiting. Hello old friend.

When I return to the studio Judas is still playing on the drum kit. He sees me and stops. My finger presses the talkback button. 'Since you're already in there, you might as well just hit each drum and I'll check the levels.'

He nods and starts on the snare. The level meter flickers with every hit, I turn a dial, keep it out of the red. But why had he phoned? Why did he feel the need to enter my life path for that brief moment? I give a thumbs up to Judas and he moves onto the bass drum. The levels bounce up and down. Why? I can feel the emptiness crying out.

A high-pitched squeal runs through the room. A feedback loop from the channel. My hand pulls the fader to zero. What the fuck was that? Judas continues to play. There's a static pop, I can smell the electricity in the air. Absent-minded I wave away the smoke rising from the console. Wait a minute; smoke shouldn't be coming out of anything. My eyes search, maybe the feedback blew a speaker. Nope, not that. Then I see it, a stream of silver smoke pouring from one of the channels.

Step away from the desk and get a technician. It's all rather exciting really. As he quickly switches off the mains power he tells me that had I touched the desk I could of got some stupid amount of voltage running through me.

I nod as I back out of the room, on my way to let Judas know. I'm laughing; I could have torched myself, I could be dead. Instead I'm laughing as I tell Judas about it.

'Fucking hell dude!' he says. 'You okay?'

'I don't think it liked your drumming.'

'Fuck dude, you realise what you've done?'

'Fucked a £300,000 mixing console.'

Now Judas laughs. 'Well, it's a good way to start the recording.'

'Yeah.' I leave him to pack away the microphones.

The technician tells me it was probably a faulty wiring that caused the problem. A loose connection that just so happened to come loose on me. So that's it. Studio shut down. No more work. After all that we had nothing we could leave with. The record button hadn't even been pressed once. Great start. It had been going so well until *he* had phoned. Like a spectre of doom his voice had seemed to curse the remainder of the night.

I sit down on a chair, letting the smell of static enter my lungs. I feel bad, what if I'd perished? His last memory would be me hanging up. My cold, emotionless 'goodbye' his mind's last reference to my voice. Why should I feel guilty though? It's not like he actually really cares. He's moved on, remember that. How stupid of me is it to think he actually still gives a fuck about me? He threw it all away. I hadn't died; I hadn't been electrocuted. Despite the obstacles this record is destined to be made. I can feel that, I can sense it will be completed. I am protected by fate. For once destiny is on my side and whilst I live under its umbrella I am invincible.

Judas enters. Everything has been boxed away. I get up and grab my bag. 'So what you plan to do for the rest of the evening instead?' he asks.

'I dunno, I might go home, have a lazy night.'

He nods as he rolls his cigarette. 'Same here, just a bit of a bummer we didn't get anything recorded.'

'Not really our fault though.' I push open the door and step into the night air. Click, flame, inhale. Euphoric smoke rushing through me. My mind focused.

'You got college tomorrow?'

'Nah, day off.'

'Cool, I gotta be in for 11.' He looks at his watch. 'Dude I gotta run so I can get the next bus.'

'Okay, I'm just gonna finish this and then head home.'

We shake our goodbyes. 'Well enjoy your quiet night.' He laughs and departs.

I lean back against the wall, inhaling deeply on the cigarette as I watch him leave. I'll enjoy it. I intend to get totally fucked.

empty

So it's time to sit down and think about everything. Something has happened and it hurts so fucking much. It's taken time to come here, to reach this point, but finally I need to clear my head.

I dunno, I just feel like I'm the only one who actually feels some sense of loss over us not being together. I miss not being able to phone him for no reason; I miss not being the first person he turns to when he needs a shoulder to cry on. I miss not being able to jump on the train and go surprise him. That's a lot of missing that I feel.

In my head when I think about it I have this nice perfect and rosy picture of it all. I hate the fact that all the plans we made aren't going to happen now. He acted like a total cunt to me at times, told me I wasn't his number one concern, hurt me so much more than anyone else in the past and yet I kept taking him back. Allowing him back into my life, knowing that there would be nights when I wouldn't be able to fucking sleep because he'd disappear off the face of the Earth without telling anyone. Always taking him back. I still want him back. He's like the little puppy bitch that shits right in front of you but you can never stop loving it.

Maybe I'm being harsh about it but when he said to meet up as mates I couldn't do it. It might be an easy jump for him to make, but to me I'm never going to be able to see him as 'just a mate'. So I told him I never wanted to see him again. I don't know if that was a good or bad idea, I was drunk at the time. Needless to say, I doubt that he's sat in his room thinking about me. What I found out proves that.

To find out that it only took under three weeks to be

replaced after everything we shared is fucking painful. It makes me feel so worthless. Did I really mean so little? And to make it worse when I phoned he lied straight to my face. 'Fuck you,' I said. 'You don't need to bullshit anymore.'

So what to do? Delete his number; you'll never need to ring it again. Take the ring from my finger; it's meaningless. But then the naked finger burns. The tears finally come, warm trails down my cheeks. The finger burns more. A broken promise, you removed the ring you promised never to not wear. The ring like the One Ring connecting me with someone. If not someone then something. A memory, a feeling. Slide the ring back on the finger.

Since finding out about his new boyfriend I've felt like shit, like I haven't known what to do with myself, like I'm walking around in limbo. Maybe I still harboured some pathetic notion that he would one day wake up and realise how much he missed me, that he needed me, that we would one day get back together and be that one complete soul again. That looks like a dream that'll never come true.

If you turn over in your mind everything, you realise how often you get lied to by society and those who mean so much to you. I don't know if can carry on producing award winning fake smiles and faux-happiness. It's draining me. I'm gradually slowing down. I feel sick for no reason.

Moments of happiness seem to be getting shorter. I'll be happy then something will knock me off my pedestal and I'll be wallowing in the dirt and nothingness I've become so accustomed to. I just want to rip out of my skin and fly away. To be happy, truly happy. To be free from the lies and the bullshit.

There had been no confusion inside of him. It was just an escape tactic. The only way in which I could be hurt so much to the point of hatred. It was a lie. Trying to make me hate was the easy option over actually telling me that I meant nothing. Knock me back into the dirt and shit then move on without a second thought. Bored of you now, need a change.

Thank you for the fun but you're no longer required. Disposable that's all I am. Use me then throw me away. Act like a spoilt brat throwing away his favourite toy in favour of the new shiny model.

I feel nothing. Empty. I'm done with trust; I'm done with care. Fuck, I can't even trust myself anymore. Looking at the almost empty vodka bottle proves it. So you wanted a catch? Well here it is. I'm self-destructive. I'm on a one man mission to destroy myself. I've fought the blackness for five years but it's getting too strong. The figure in the shadows is slowly rebuilding his strength.

I don't know if what I'm doing is right, well, things like meaningless sex don't feel right to me. I dunno. It's all fucked up. It's a mess. Well, not a mess, it's a situation. I think and care about the feelings of someone who doesn't feel the same for me. Tick tock… tick tock. Time's ticking.

I stand up; sway a little. Maybe I'm a bit drunk, but not as fucked as I'm gonna be. Pull on my coat and head out the house. Walking out into the night, vitamin K in my pocket. Time to find a nice quiet place to be alone.

Okay, so I'm fucking myself up with drugs, what's the big deal? At what cost? Fuck it, I'll work those out later.

007

C$_{13}$H$_{16}$NCIO

Ha, what have I done? I mean it could be a nice choice of location, hidden, dark, safe, everything you would want but only if I wasn't surrounded by stone slabs carved with names of those since departed. Yep, I'm sat on my ass, back against a tree in a graveyard, and my limbs refuse to move. *Why bother?* they say, *it's so comfortable here.*

I'm giggling at the stupidity of it all. Last time I'd been outside the castle ruins, a much friendlier place. I manage to raise my hand to rub my face. It soon falls back to the ground, letting gravity guide it. I stare into the shadows, a flash, a flicker of light. I cock my head and frown. Another flash, moving, guiding itself between the gravestones. Approaching slowly.

A whisper, a breath against my ear. My gaze still stares forward. I'm not scared, call me crazy but I'm sure you're meant to sense a little bit of apprehension when some invisible entity breathes sweet nothings into your ear. But I fear nothing. Peace. Silence. A voice from the grave.

'Come with me,' it whispers. 'Let me take you by the hand, guide you.'

'I dunno, I've got to get home at some point.'

'Don't worry, I'll protect you. There are things I need to show you. Things you must consider.'

I let it grip my hand. A stranger of vapour taking me, leading me as we walk in the darkness. A space of nothing, realm between realms, no mans land of the soul. All around me shadows move within shadows. Watching, smiling. I'm doing the right thing. I feel safe, all fears fading, melting away, leaving a multicoloured trail behind me, my connection with the real world, the ball of string used to guide me out of the Minotaur's lair.

In the distance, approaching closer with each step is a door, painted white. We reach it, nailed to its front are the numbers 220504, a meaning hidden within my mind. Without being told I reach for it. I can sense the phantom stranger standing behind me.

'Go in, go through,' he whispers. 'Don't look back.'

'Are you coming in as well?' I ask, my eyes transfixed on the numbers in front of me.

'I can go no further. Here I must stay in wait for you. This is something that must be done alone.'

My hand pulls the handle and pushes the door open. A swirling portal of lights and colours fill the empty space. Moving constantly, interweaving, blending, shining out in the darkness. I step forward, allowing myself to be engulfed by it, let the colours blend into mine, becoming one. I hear the door slam shut. I'm falling.

I'm speeding through a tunnel, falling through its centre, dragged down by gravity. A splash, an explosion of colour, rainbows merging with water, erupting into the air, a stone thrown into an ocean.

I'm sitting in a bath tub, naked, warm water around me. My hand raises and I look at it in confusion. A giggle. I'm smiling but the giggle isn't mine. I look up; sharing the bath with me is Sam. He's smiling, clear as day, beautiful.

'Why did you do that?' He laughs, a sweet laughter.

'I dunno.' What the fuck? Where am I? No, stupid question, I know where I am, but why am I here? This is finished business, isn't it?

'Fool,' he says.

I stand, getting out of the bath. 'I've had enough, I'm going to dry myself off.'

'Okay. I'm gonna stay in a little longer.'

'That's cool,' I say, wrapping a towel around my waist and padding my way through to his bedroom. Everything crystal clear. Real, just as I remember it. I walk over to the bed and sit down. Drying myself, pulling on my boxers and jeans. Remain seated, leant forward with my head resting in my hands. Why have they brought me here?

'You okay?'

I look up, Sam's stood in front of me, towel wrapped around him. 'Yeah, I'm okay.' I smile. This is how it should be, glimpses of our happy times. How we were, our everyday associations. No arguments, no anger.

'I love you,' he says.

I wish I knew that for sure. I wish I knew he meant it. I want to believe it. I know it was true once. That's the memory I should hold on to. 'I love you too.'

He smiles, I rise and we hug. Hug each other tightly. I can feel both of us crying, tears rolling down our naked backs, warm. Being pulled into each other. The rings on our fingers burning bright. A glowing white light, merging, extending. A lightning flash rushes up my arm, striking my heart, our hearts. We're spinning, round and round, faster, the scenery blurs. Our bodies becoming one. Sealing together, becoming a part of each other forever. A bond through a silver band, a connection between two souls.

The spinning stops, I'm alone. The darkness all around me. The door closed firmly in front of my face. I throw myself at it, trying to force it open but it's locked. Bolted securely. I fall against it, sliding to the floor, salty tears running down my face.

'Did you see? Did you learn? Did you remember?' The whisper.

I look up but see nothing, a shadow hiding in the shadows. 'Why?' I shout. 'Why the fuck did you do that?'

I feel a phantom hand on my shoulder, calming, understanding. 'You were in danger of losing sight. Forgetting the small moments you two shared. Forgetting the everyday minutes you cherished, replacing them with anger, choosing the fights and coldness as a way of justifying. Remember your promise; remember him as he was, as you truly feel. It'll be harder that way; it'll hurt you more than hatred. Remember your love for him and learn to deal with the separation. He loved you like you did him, cherish that.'

I'm smiling, crying. Sadness and love merging painfully. So this is remembrance.

The voice continues. 'You can't judge on what you are not part of. Let him go follow his path to happiness, if what he felt was true, one day he will return, will once again stand at your side. Hatred will prevent this. You must see clearly with your heart.'

I feel myself being lifted. Carried through the darkness, spasms running through my body, tears flowing. Crystal rivers pouring from my eyes, dropping slowly to the floor. Silver splatters coating the darkness. A path through this pain. Remember the silver, let it guide you.

We're retracing the path we came, my body reabsorbing the multicoloured string left to guide. Pulling myself back to reality, filling my body with substance.

I sit up sharply. The graveyard lit by the glow of dawn. The first touches of sunshine awakening. I pull myself to my feet, pulling my coat tighter around me. I've got work to do, bands to sort out, an album to record, and at some point piece myself back together. To be reborn we need to destroy what we've become. Good morning. A new day dawning.

Ooh, a little red button with 'self destruct' written on it. I wonder what happens if I just push it.

Push.

Done, let's wait for the end of days.

victims of the state

Essay

'You're being lied to.' An opening statement like that would have been a grand gesture but only if I believed in it. Well, I do believe it as I feel we *are* being told lies, but to focus in on such a small part of the grand picture would be stupid, it would be too easy. The core problem we face is not that we are being lied to, but that we are being mislead. Yes, falsehoods and lies do play a large part in the misleading, but so does distorted and selective quoting of facts. Facts aren't lies, but facts mislead.

It's easy to see through a lie. We know that we are told lies by those we elect to govern over us, and we are usually quick to stand up and complain when these falsehoods are brought to our attention. Yet most of us will follow blindly a fact that has been worded in such a way to make a political point. We see or hear the word 'fact' and instantly agree with it and never stop to question the motivation behind why it was used. It's this herd mentality that disgusts me. We live in a democracy, we have the freedom to question and call to account what we see as wrong, yet an individual will not stand up and speak out unless he can be a hidden face amongst the larger crowds. Don't get me wrong, I know that this is not the case for everyone, but it cannot be denied that the distinct majority will sit in silence, take their freedoms for granted and wait until someone else will speak out for them. That is, of course, only if that someone doesn't go against the 'facts' they have chosen to believe.

This is the problem with all aspects of the society we are forced to accept. Whether we like it or not, all dissension or resentment towards the accepted 'norm' is frowned upon.

Those who have an unrestrained spirit are actively silenced, removed from public attention, or ordered to conform. Extreme emotions are shunned under the belief that such tendencies must be confronted without question. People who act upon their beliefs become outcasts, people who must be ignored or despised. Fair enough, if these beliefs are acted out in extreme and childish ways which result in the needless loss of innocent lives then I will stand up with you all in my disgust and want for retribution, but let us not forget that extremists often act upon a belief that has been distorted to fit themselves; they act on falsehoods, misled guiding and misinformation. They act out a lie in a manner that solves nothing. However, it is ludicrously preposterous to prevent someone from having a say if it is structured in an intelligent and well-informed manner. A criticism of a process allows for investigation and the verification of *fact*.

If more people opened their eyes, looked outside of their comfortable existence and questioned, then maybe, just maybe, it will instigate a change for the better. Yet, as with most things in these modern days, the fire has gone out of people's hearts. They merely move like machines as they go about their daily chores. They exist as silent cogs in the big machine that makes up the regime. The regime that has allowed the expansion of the monster that is Globalisation. All it takes is for one strong cog to ask that fateful question 'why?' to cause an error that causes other cogs to stop working. That's why governments hate those who are different; those who go against the grain. They cause the system to malfunction and as a result need to be silenced.

The most damaging aspect that has entered into the doctrines of modern governments is this stupid notion of political correctness - a belief that enforces the state's morals in the most dogmatic and rabid manner. It is an extremist view that forces morals and ideals onto everyone regardless of personal feelings. It clouds judgments and at its very basic level is telling us, no, *instructing* us on what we can or can't say, who we have to like and what we have to do in order to be an acceptable member of society. Does that sound like a democracy to you? To live under a government that tells you how to live your life, who you have the right to discriminate, and how long you have to waste your life as a cog in the system. Here's the problem. That is what a modern democracy is. The modern democracy is a brainwashed state where the people follow their government blindly like sheep. The modern democracy is little more than an acceptable faced totalitarian state of the likes we spent the last century trying to eradicate, yet we still don't question it. And like all of those totalitarian regimes, they inflict and force their way of life on people and other nations without choice or reason. That to me is an essential wrong. When a government starts telling people what they can or can't do to their own bodies then that is a regime far worse than that imposed on Germany under Adolf Hitler.

You may try to defend a democracy through its notion of equality of people but I'm going to put the cards on the table now and say that that is another misguided opinion. In fact whenever I hear people spouting on about everyone's equality, I just want to pop each and every one of those reality bubbles that fester around their heads so that maybe they can hear the absurdity of the propagandist shit they defecate with every word they say. If everyone is equal then what right does anyone have to make sections of the society outcasts? Just because someone chooses to smoke, for example, what right does anyone have to deny them of that privilege? People scream on about the dangers of 'passive' smoking but let's look at it from outside your comfort zone. Walk down the street and breathe; at any moment as many as 5 to 10 cars will pass by, each pumping hundreds, if not thousands, of times more deadly chemicals per second into the atmosphere than your humble smoker. You all breath this in without complaint, and why? Because your government doesn't say it's wrong.

If you can't see the misuse of information or the lies; if you jump on the bandwagon without question; or, more importantly, you don't ask 'why?' then you are all blind. You are corroding the rights and freedoms of others just through that belief in the dogma of equality which you grasp so desperately yet totally misunderstand. The nation's 'equality' is not equal rights, but equal rights for those who toe the governmental line. I don't subscribe to any notion of equality, but I however find it blindingly insulting to the freedoms of a person to deny them the right to do to their body whatever they like. And just for the record, if you're about to believe that because I don't believe in any form of equality that I am abhorrently racist or whatever, let me make a statement of fact. I don't see differences in the colour of skin, sexuality or creed, to me to even do so is a reference to a notion that there is an important difference.

You're all being misled and I doubt that any of you probably care, or if you do, you'll just wait until someone else raises that point for you. This is a notion that I find disturbing. How after everything we have witnessed throughout history can you sit without complaint and just rot under a government you claim to hate? Your apathy is destroying your will power; your vision is clouded. But you're happy to be sheep; happy to part of the herd; happy to be led to slaughter without so much as a whimper. I'm happy for you, but whilst you spread the government's shit over the toast you feed your children, the time has come. I'm here to have my say whether you like it or not.

a breakfast of pills – $C_9H_{13}N$

I'm fucked up. Totally fucked up. I fuck my head and then proceed to fuck everything else up. I destroy everything and this time I want it to be the last. The final explosion. I will destroy myself to make this statement, this art. I will go for broke, hold no stops. Bang! This is The Red Devil Incident. That is my legacy.

I've broken all the rules I put into place. Rules I have insisted upon for years. Never turn up to a band practice drunk, never record when off your face. All those   lie naked and bruised on the side of the road, knocked over and left for dead by my speeding car. I can't help but smile as no one has noticed, it's just Dom being slightly more crazy than usual. But why should they be able to tell, despite all the amounts of amphetamines coursing through me I never miss a beat, always in time. Listen to the sound of my war drums.

Don't you find it somewhat depressing that it has come to this? I'm not really portraying myself at my best am I? My life is fast falling into a routine. Wake up. Pub. College. Pub. Studio. Home. Bed. Then you get days like today. Days where I have a gourmet breakfast of amphetamines. Make a good role model don't I?

I'm always professional, you may disagree with me, but the first track from the album is coming along perfectly. I always record the opening track first, it sets the tone for what follows, the most important track on the CD. What an opener, a track trying to awaken that secret thought in people's minds, to make them doubt. *Don't you see your soul's been sold to work away these endless days?* 'Victims of the State' the battle cry of RDI.

That's the only thing keeping me going, this album. It feels like my only purpose, my goal, my life. It seems too weird saying that so early on, but it's like a baby, you nurture, protect, watch it grow and love every part of it. It's a journey. A journey for me and a journey for The Red Devil Incident. God, I'm rambling.

I'm buzzing away. My back and arm feel like they're on fire but it's all good. Fuck I'm such a fuck up. Eating pills for breakfast, what the fuck? This is Dom. I am Dom. Meh.

I tried to write a new tune today, it didn't go well. It was too bouncy, tripped out. Fucked up semi classical. Modern classical, discordant and rampant. I shouldn't turn on my computer when I'm alone, down and high. I do stupid things like send e-mails telling someone who foolishly fancies me to fuck off and leave me alone. Well, not that I could actually give a fuck about their feelings. He's nothing more than a cow faced loser with no dreams for the future, an entity just existing until the day he dies, and what a hollow death that would be for him, he believes in nothing after life. Let his corpse turn to mud and let his soul mourn his close-minded wasted existence. As you no doubt gathered, I'm not the sort of person you want to be around at the moment.

It's not so bad now; I'm on my way down, which is lucky as Judas is meant to be coming round soon. I was dreading him calling but he thankfully called late in the day. My speech had still been a little too fast but maybe he didn't notice. I speak quickly anyway. Plenty of time to get my head sorted and think back about what I've done today, which is virtually next to nothing having been locked in my room bouncing off the walls.

I feel my thumb start scratching at the top of my middle finger. An old habit that dies hard. The comedown. The slow stumble to reality. Saucer eyes slowly reacting as normal. In this one moment you realise how fucking lonely you are, it's only for a moment but it burns like a cigarette burn on your chest. It burns because to release the anger you extinguished your cancer stick out on yourself, just above the right nipple. Breathe. Calm. Relax. Better put a t-shirt on. Judas will be here any minute.

As if on cue with my thoughts, the doorbell rings. Judas has arrived. I rush downstairs and pull open the door. 'Hey dude,' I say excitedly.

'Hey.' He smiles and enters, wiping his feet on the mat like he always does. 'How's it going?'

My mouth opens. 'A little bit crazy. If I seem a bit out of it, well, there's a reason. I've got a confession to make.' I laugh, why the fuck am I telling him this shit? He's my best friend but does he really need to know?

'What's that dude?'

'I ate amphetamines for breakfast and I'm just on the last bit of comedown.'

He laughs. 'That's cool dude, I just had a joint so I'm pretty much the same.' And that's why I like him. He never judges you on what you've done. That's why I trust him so much.

'So, how's your day been?' I ask as we enter my room.

'Lazy, not had much to do. You know how it is. So how's RDI sounding?'

'It's sounding pretty fucking sweet.' It's nice to know it's genuine interest. 'I have a really good feeling about it all.'

'Yeah, me too. I was playing the tracks today on guitar. 'Revolution #h8' is a fucking awesome riff.'

'Thanks dude.' As Judas sits on the bed to roll a joint, I smile. 'You pick the DVD, I'll go grab the beers.'

2005
OCTOBER

a breakfast of nicotine

Early October, still early days. Full of hope and determination. I would venture to say that I'm happy, whether or not that's a true statement or just drugs blocking me from thinking I don't know but it's still a good feeling. I know I've been employing displacement activities lately, finding stupid things to do instead of sitting down and concentrating on pushing forward. The Red Devil Incident is my only concern; it's engulfing me, pulling me under its saving spell.

I'd intended on going into London today but instead I found myself in my second home with Judas and the rest. Sat around the crowded table, pint glasses and cigarette butts decorating the wooden surface. Dom, Judas, Bunny and Ward. The gang, the unit. Mates at varying levels, well, if I'm honest I've never truly classed Ward as a friend, he's always been the forgettable entity within the group. Bunny's the new boy, the latest addition. It started with Judas and I, then the rest attached themselves. Dom the ringleader, it's nice to feel admired.

We spent the night catching up properly. It's the first time for months since we last sat here. Clear up the business from the past and look towards the future. To think this had been put on hold for a year as I spent almost every waking hour with Sam. I don't feel guilty about neglecting my friends but at least they're still around, still speaking.

As I walked home alone in the autumn night air, I felt fresh, alive, invigorated. When you live somewhere for so long it all becomes the same, your appreciation drops and you start to get complacent. Tonight it felt like the first time I walked through the streets. When you hang around with your best mates you realise that everything isn't actually that bad, you ignore the shadows and overcast dreams and simply exist for the now. Maybe that's why mankind is so weary, spending each day thinking about the great unknown blank of the future rushing towards us. Infinite possibilities dragging us towards our graves. I'm walking the path I've made, there's no going back now.

The week passes with its usual monotony. A routine I've fallen into. I see Judas every day, our bond of friendship returning to how it used to be. But the routine; has it come to this so soon in the year?

Wednesday. Pub. Drink. Laugh. An endless stream of random conversations, mouths constantly moving. Say goodbyes. Buy coke. Cut. Line. Snort. Drink more. Bed.

Thursday. Wake up. Shower. Meet Judas at the pub. Studio. Home. Bed. At least the drums are almost completely recorded.

Now it's Saturday morning, I'm lying in bed with a pain in my stomach. Freshly awoken hypochondriac thoughts rushing through my head. I curl into a foetal ball. Squeeze tighter together; try to dislodge the mysterious pain. Fuck it, I wanna scream, shout, rip my fingers deep into my stomach and pull the offending object out.

Crawl out from under the duvet, stand uneasily and shuffle to the mirror. My eyes focus and I groan openly. I look like shit. Disturbed sleep leaving its dark shade at the corners of my eyes. Then it hits me. Looking at my naked reflection three observations scream into existence. I haven't eaten for forty hours, I haven't showered for forty-eight hours, I haven't shaved for one hundred and sixty-eight hours.

Fall backwards onto the bed. Reach for my tobacco. Roll, lick, seal. Time to sort out those observations in order of importance. Click, flame, inhale. A breakfast of nicotine and tar before I get dressed and guide my skinny frame to the local overpriced convenience store for food and alcohol. Judas is coming round later so I'd better get the beers in.

once again...

...we find ourselves in the pub. Judas and I sat opposite sides of a table talking away, his pint of beer and my vodka and orange stood upon the wooden surface alongside the graveyard of empty glasses and cigarette butts. We'd come for a quiet drink but now we've found ourselves invited to help someone celebrate their birthday, how could we not say 'yes'? So after our pre-invite ordered food is devoured we leave one pub for the sanctuary of another, taking money out of my bank I'll be set for wherever this night leads us.

When we arrive at the next pub we manoeuvre our way over to the established group of friends and sit down. Judas goes to the bar, it's his round. Double vodka and orange for me. Sit. Roll. Ignite. I smoke too much, not that I care about that, it's just something I always think. A social chaining of cancer, well okay, not that bad, I've seen worse. Breathe in deeply then exhale the trail of smoke into the atmosphere. All around the table others do the same.

In another room a band's playing. Live noise bleeding through the walls, merging chaotically with the CD playing in some distant corner behind a bar. So much noise, conversations, band, CD, my mind blurs, I can feel it pushing down on me. Claustrophobia. Drag on the cigarette, I know what's coming next, the disconnected dreamlike feeling, waiting for someone to click their fingers to awake me from some confused dream. I know it's coming because it always does, a flashback fear born from two figures trapped on a crowded tube train, psilocybin coursing through their systems. When you've opened your mind so many times nothing is ever the same. A lost daydream confuses with reality and you wait to be awoken.

A glass appears in front of me, my thoughts snap back, clear and precise. Judas sits next to me and reaches for my tobacco, he knows he doesn't have to ask.

'Dude,' he says. 'The queue for the fucking bar was massive, and some stupid blonde bitch pushed in front of me.'

I laugh. 'I take it she had a massive order.'

'Like she was buying for the whole pub.' He sparks his cigarette to life and sits back. 'Quite nice in here.'

I look around, having not paid attention to my surroundings; it's the first time I've ever been in here. Four years and I've only really ever drunk in the same pub. You can live in a place for years and not even know certain things exist. 'Yeah, I'll agree with you on that one.' I smile, lift my glass to my lips and drink. I have no respect for my alcohol; I drink screwdrivers like they are plain orange. So like me, take but never relax enough to enjoy.

'So how's the RDI mixing coming along?'

'Well, there's not much more I can do now until we get working on your guitar parts.'

Judas takes a swig of his drink. 'I was practicing some of the parts yesterday. I still really love 'Revolution'.'

I smile and light up another cigarette. I'm not going to comment, my ego doesn't allow me. I know it's a good tune but I'm not going swimming up my own ass, that's not what I do. I let my eyes flick around the pub as I bring my drink to my lips. Crowded, full of smiling faces. Visions of friendship and happiness. The glass is returned to the table empty. So this is what friendship has become. Alcohol, cigarettes and constant repetitive small talk. Maybe that makes me sound harsh but when I go out to enjoy myself I don't want to talk about work, I want a break, to not think about what I need to do or achieve. I want to simply have fun without care.

Judas continues. 'We're recording 'Victims' first right?'

I nod. 'Yeah we start guitars next week now we've got almost all the drum parts down. So the first tracks are

'Victims', 'Revolution' and 'Falling Down'. So I guess it's just get those sorted.'

'Cool, I'm really looking forward to it.'

I eye up my empty glass, noticing Judas' is empty too. 'Another drink?'

'Yeah, okay then. You want me to order?'

'Erm, it's up to you. Think you can handle the crowds?'

'Yeah, I think I'll make it.'

Smiling I hand him a £10 note. 'Same again dude.'

He nods, takes the money and disappears into the swarms of people.

More people have joined our table, all involved with their own conversations. So many different lives, crossing each other's paths briefly then moving on. They play their part in your life for such a small amount, a month, a year, two years, and then you all move on. Distant memories in a sea of new experiences.

I turn in my seat and see Shelby sat alone on a table behind me. I spin my chair round so it faces his. 'Alright dude?' I say.

'Hey Dom, how's it going?' Someone generally pleased to see me.

'You know, the usual.'

So we talk, not much to catch up on really, we see each other virtually every week. Thankfully, blissfully no mention of my work. I roll myself another cigarette, I'm chaining, maybe I've thought that already but I can't be bothered trying to remember. 'What I really want,' I say aloud without noticing it, 'is a fucking line.'

Shelby's conversation stumbles, I look up and he's simply staring at me. He knows and I know it's what we both really want. 'Random,' he says.

A glass hits the table in front of me, a double vodka and orange. I look up, it's Judas; he places my change in my hand with a smile. 'Hey dude,' he says to Shelby.

Click, flame, inhale. I light the cigarette as my tobacco

is lifted from in front of me by Judas. 'I think everyone's heading to Time later,' he continues.

'Cool,' I offer. I know what's coming.

'Dude we should go, it'll be a laugh.'

'Yeah okay, you wanna crash at mine so you don't have to rush off?' Told you I knew what was coming, I knew I'd offer that, not that it's a problem, just that I don't know whether or not I've left a line resting in front of my computer screen. Doubt it though, but not to worry, it's easy to move out of sight.

'Yeah, that'll be awesome. I'll go tell them we're gonna go.' He rises, lights his fag and disappears from view.

My attention returns to Shelby.

'I can get anything,' he says.

'Anything?'

'Yeah, I'm getting myself £200 worth of coke. I'll halve it with you if you want. £100 each.'

I nod, I'm not thinking the offer over in my head, he said 'anything', now that's tempting. 'Anything?'

'Yeah I just said.'

'Get me heroin.' It's blunt; it falls from my mouth like lead.

He pauses, doesn't say a word.

'If you can get anything, get me heroin.'

'I can do that, but what about the coke?'

'If you can get me heroin then fuck cocaine. Find out how much it'll cost and I'll get it.'

'Okay. You sure? Or just joking?'

My eyes look directly into his. 'I'm sure.'

He nods. Judas returns. I pick up my glass and drink.

The night rolls on, conversations, double vodkas, cigarettes. Shelby leaves early, Judas disappears and I'm left having to speak to people I don't really have an interest talking to. Just nod your head at the right moment and they think you're listening. Self obsessed no ones with their 'me me' conversations. No point talking about yourself, they don't care, besides which I really hate talking about myself.

It's not that I'm ashamed of who I am that I avoid speaking about myself, it's just I don't waste my breath talking to people who don't truly care, who are just being courteous whilst waiting for a pause long enough to return the topic back to them. The thing I've learnt over the years is that I generally find myself surrounded by these self-centred people, you know the type, 'listen to our problems and help us, but please don't burden us with yours.' It's no surprise to me then that here I am listening - or not as the case may be - to an endless stream of bullshit on a night when I was supposed to be enjoying myself. Shit happens I guess.

Empty glass in front of me. I rise and move towards the bar. God bless alcohol. When I return with my drink, Judas is sat waiting. I smile as I approach.

'We'll be heading off in about half an hour,' he informs me.

'Cool, gives me plenty of time to drink this.'

Conversation, drink, smoke. Time flies by so quickly, so blissfully that before I know it it's time for us to move on. Leave the pub and out into the open air.

We're headed towards some club; it's a rock night apparently. I'm laughing, despite my disgust for clinging sycophants I'm having a good time. Dom and Judas, drunk and prating around. Good times, memories to add to the library of your life. So many adventures already experienced on this street we're walking up. Happy.

We arrive, pay to get in, run to the bar. Two pints of cider and we're sorted. Music blares and I spot Shelby, walk over to him. Everyone's drunk, no one gives a shit. Judas spits his drink over me, I remove my cap and head-butt him, he punches me in the stomach. Pointless fun, no anger involved. Funny to think that the first year we met we disliked each other, friendship born out of a mutual dislike for some ego filled twat. Best friends for three years without a single argument. That's what you call friendship.

Fuelled by alcohol the night rolls on sweetly, sweeter with Shelby's agreement to get me an appointment with Doctor Brownstone. The evening's end almost in sight until I see Judas having a few words with another guy, heated words. Judas appears at my side. 'If that guy speaks to me again,' he says. 'I'm gonna floor him.'

'What'd he say?'

'I'll tell you later, it's not important.' Sound's ominous doesn't it? I sip the remainder of my cider.

Here we are walking home. Judas' fuming away at my side. He's angry. We've just had a run in with the guy he argued with in the club. I sorted it out although his friend was a fucking bigger twat that I almost head-butted. All that hassle because Judas had danced with a girl, one of our friends, who he knew full well had a boyfriend. This cunt head had made such a big issue over some insignificant meaningless fun, even the boyfriend found it hilarious. Not to worry, we'll get into mine and have our usual post drinking ritual. A cup of tea and two slices of toast each. It's a habit we've acquired over the years but it's something we adhere to each time. If we come home early the ritual changes, we drink Jack D and Coke from the bottle that sits in my room. The bottle no one else is allowed to touch. It's Judas' and mine only.

Arrive home; I leave Judas in the kitchen as I run upstairs to grab my cup. I look around the room quickly. There isn't a random line anywhere to be seen.

divas and drums

The drums are complete, the basis of all the main tracks laid down. The foundations of the album in place. It was a surreal moment as the stop button was pressed for the last time on the drums. Stage one complete, breathe a sigh of relief, we're on track, despite everything the schedule is still in place. Thankfully.

I was bouncing off the walls though but *shh* don't tell anybody. Judas is unaware that for most of these sessions I've been off my face. Told you I was a professional. The click track played and I stuck to it; I've always been pretty good with metronomes.

So yeah, my performance side of this recording is over now until we do some vocal guides, but for the next few sessions I get to sit back and just produce. Not much of a break given I have to edit and mix in every bit of my spare time, but still you know what I mean. I hope.

I had an argument with the guy who was using the smaller studio and second live room. We call him Malta Man; all he writes is cheesy Eurovision pop, Industrial comes before that anytime. Well, there was me drumming away mid-take and he bursts into the live room declaring I had no right to record drums when he was attempting to record vocals. I think my exact words were 'and you're telling me because I care? Just fuck off out my live room.'

He didn't look too happy.

Then as Judas and I were listening back to a take in the studio, the door opens and this troll faced thing walks in and starts mouthing off about how important she thinks she is and that we had no right ruining her session. She was really going for it, flapping arms, rampant head bobbing. Pure diva strop. Finally she shut up.

I looked at Judas then turned back to look at her face so laughably filled with indignation. 'Have you quite finished dear?' I said calmly. 'To act like a fucking diva you need to at least have an ounce of talent.'

She opened her mouth to reply, I pressed play and the drums beat it shut. She stormed from the room and we just pissed ourselves laughing. The session carried on.

I'm quite harsh when it comes down to it, but still, no one tells me I can't record this fucking album. The fact that the faux-diva repeatedly gave me the evils for the rest of the night just made stage one's completion that little bit more satisfying.

interlude in the rain

I'm walking, thinking. It's night, dark and lamp lit. I'm just walking around with my iPod on shuffle, a computer choosing my life's soundtrack at random. I've been walking around aimless and without direction. Exploring areas of Guildford I've never ventured near. A sailor on a journey across the sea. Columbus discovered the Americas, I discovered Charlotteville.

I sit myself down on a bench in Stoke Park. My randomised play-list in sync with my mind; mirroring my feelings. Sit and sigh. Deep, long sigh. Close the eyes, there's nothing worth focusing on. Something is niggling, I don't know what it is. Soul deep with a cancer growing ready to burst out and let its presence be known, but not yet, not now.

It starts to rain. Drops of water from the sky breaking on contact with my body. I remain seated, feeling the cold tears of Heaven beat against me. I look out into the dark, around me the vast expanse of open space. One solitary figure. Alone. Alone in more ways than one.

I'm moved. There's nothing like crying in the rain as the Black Eyed Pea's 'Shut up' plays. I don't know why I'm crying. There's no reason for it but still they come. Warm tears of humanity mixing with the cold tears of divine abandon. Maybe I'm so engrossed in my work that I need to let out some subconscious part of my brain that I choose to ignore. It isn't a full-blown breakdown; I just let the tears run down my cheeks as I stare forward with glazed eyes.

Wash away the pain and dirt and you're left clean. Refreshed. Say your silent prayers into the cosmos and wait for eternity to reply.

red-eyed

01 November 2005

It's 11:12am. Mark's sleeping on the floor and I'm sat writing away at a journal entry. We got in a 7:30 this morning, a good twelve hours since we left the house yesterday following smoking a fucking massive weed tulip Mark made and had waiting when I walked in from college. It was pretty much smoke, shower, get ready, leave.

I'd decided what a wonderful idea it would be to wear only a ripped up t-shirt which showed one of my nipples with its piercing, and a lot of my waist, with blue jeans. That was it. It was alright to begin with, namely when I was walking but standing on an open train station smoking a cigarette it started looking like a slight mistake. At least the train was warm.

I haven't said where we went have I? A club in London. *Red Eye* at the Ghetto, a grotty, rather lacklustre place where I once got kicked, no dragged out of after getting too drunk and pushing the bouncer out of my way. That was also the night that I went on to attack Sam on the way home.

So yeah, night went as usual, drunk too much, we both did; then I disappeared off to the toilets with some random person who all I remember had a green t-shirt on but yeah, use your imagination to picture what went on in the cubical. It was an alright night. Saw some people I knew, faces from the not so distant past. The problems came when the club closed. It was fucking freezing; I chose to go dressed in a sluttish ripped up t-shirt so I only have myself to blame. We found warmth outside some restaurant's air vents so we sat there for a while huddled against it, warming ourselves with greasy smelling air. Then it blew out cold so we had to move on, Mark rattling on beside me about it being a big conspiracy against us.

Waterloo, glorious Waterloo station. I have a love/hate relationship with this station. So many happy meetings, so many reluctant goodbyes, so many memories. It was 4:49 when we walked into the station; I know this as I had a photo on my camera proving that to be the case. Quite a few photos actually. Photographic evidence that I did indeed cover myself with the newspaper like a tramp and it wasn't merely some random dream I had.

We scrabbled together some money for a coffee between us and went and sat down as we waited a fucking hour for a train. 5:45 jumped on the train, fell asleep within moments. Guildford, walked home in the freezing cold, drunk half a cup of tea then fell asleep. Which brings us nicely and concisely back to the start. Me sat here writing in a journal.

I've got college in a few hours. Two hours of *Music Media and Marketing*, fun. I feel a bit guilty, Mark's ill, a random chill he's caught. He had it last night but carried on partying. That's what you call a true professional, even if he's paying for it now.

I feel rough; I'm going to shower and tart myself up, powder my nose in the bathroom if you catch my drift.

I'll buy us chips for dinner.

The week ambles by. I love it when bro is down visiting, the time flies by so quickly, and for once I actually allow myself a break in work. There's not much worth showing him on the RDI front, safe for a few mixed drum tracks and basic synth guides. 'Victims' sounds good but will be even better once the guitars have been added to it.

So it reached Saturday and Mark has totally recovered from his random fever - I doped him out on sleeping pills and flu capsules that seemed to do the trick. We're currently walking to the corner shop for some reason, I can't actually remember why we're doing this, I think we need some more tobacco, but most likely Mark just needs some more Rizla. I'm sure we'll remember when we walk in.

For breakfast today we had two amphetamine filled capsules, so that's starting to get digested in the stomach, its kiss being rushed into our systems. Mark caught me swallowing them so I felt it was only right that I should give my last two to him. Let's call this 'experimenting', I haven't told him I do this quite a bit at the moment - read as a lot. As far as I am concerned he knows as much as he needs to, not that he would react in any way, it's just not important to tell him. We're grinning like a pair of Cheshire Cats as we enter the shop. I grab myself a chocolate bar. I'm fucking hungry; he orders the tobacco. We pay, we leave, we walk home.

It starts to kick in.

Fourteen hours later and we reach the tail end, the effects fading, leaving a dull thud in the head, a slight disconnection from reality, like a small membrane surrounding the body. My fingers tingle, well itch like a motherfucker from bad speed I guess, and I got the good old habit of thumb scratching the tip of the middle finger. I spoke for nine hours, constantly and without break. I feel sorry for Mark having to endure that, he just sat there listening to me telling him what his problems are. I mean I wasn't horrible about it, they were just general observations but at the end of the day what right do I have to mention other people's problems when I won't even mention my own?

We both cried to the demo of our track 'Sleep', it's instrumental at the moment so I sat there and sung. The lyrics mean so much, I sang and broke down whilst singing, he broke down whilst listening. 'You know Dom,' Mark had said. 'I sometimes cry about how close I came to losing you, and how nobody was listening to you and didn't care. That was fucked up.'

I couldn't speak, how do you comeback to a revelation like that? Dom speechless? Something that doesn't happen too often. Then he closed his eyes. I freaked out. 'Open your eyes,' I shouted.

'Why?' He opens them.

'Don't ever close your eyes on me when you're off your face.'

'Dom, I only…'

'Just don't fucking do it.' I hate it; it scares me; so easy to slip from conscious to un. With closed eyes you can never tell, they could die and you wouldn't notice. Eyes are the mirrors to the soul, I need to see them, need to seem them move, need to see the life within them, and the messages they send. So much can be prevented if you read the messages the eyes speak. Darkness lays behind closed eyes. The never ending darkness that surrounds us all, waiting to welcome us with open arms. You pick up habits, fears, when you walk through the mirror, certain things you focus on to maintain a link with the real world. My link is the eyes of whoever I'm tripping with; it's a habit, just like this infernal scratching. I know tomorrow my finger's going to be sore.

At least Mark enjoyed himself, it passed the day, we wouldn't have done much anyway. Click, flame, inhale. I've only had a few cigarettes today so that's good. People say I should give up anyway as it's bad for me. I dunno, the slight cough I get every now and again seems to do the same amount of work for my stomach as sit-ups do, plus it's easier, I can smoke at the same time.

Seriously though my smoking should be the least of their worries. I'm on the road to self destruction and none of them have even noticed. It's like toxic anorexia, they won't realise until it's too late, I will have crashed, burnt and be ready for rebirth. That's when you'll see who truly cares for you. God, I'm a bundle of laughs ain't I. Adjust face, smile. Behind the mask of happiness no one will see the shattered shards fall to the ground.

Ever look at a photo taken one year and compared it to one taken on exactly that day the year previous? I've just done that, how surreal to see that I'm wearing exactly the same clothes in each, only this year I'm not running around the Natural History museum, instead I find myself in the pub having slept through a lecture and walked out early. How life changes yet endlessly stays the same.

loneliness rising

So I'm trying to be honest here, write my thoughts, experiences, what I've learnt. If I'm honest, I don't know where I'm headed. Down and down in a spiral. I just want to lock myself away and work, finish what I've started and not have to smile these stupid fucking smiles each day. I'm not connecting; I can feel my legs being grabbed at, this fucking world trying to pull my feet to the ground. What would I see in reality? A world of shit destroying everything it touches. These lines, these pills, this brain keep me going when my body just wants to crumble to the ground with a rope around its neck. So much pain, deceit and anger, all this disposal of me must be for a purpose right? There must be *a* reason, it can't be all for nothing. There has to be one, doesn't there?

I've noticed a growing disdain for this world, its people marching on with no cares, locked in self-interest. I can only connect with those I find worthy of my respect; everyone else can rot in the pond they exist in for all I care. I met this guy; he was nineteen years old and had absolutely no personality at all. It depressed me because here's me, twenty two with a persona I've tried so hard to maintain, I struggled to be *me* and there in front of me was some pathetic creature who simply hangs on everyone's word, modifying his personality to fit in with those around him.

We were, as usual, sat in the pub and once all my mates had dispersed, I was left alone to finish my drink with this guy. Don't get me wrong, I didn't just judge him straight out, I actually made the effort to speak to him and it was like getting blood out of a fucking stone. I'd start a conversation and he'd be all staring away into the distance with some dumb-ass look on his face, then I'd fall quiet and turn away to prevent myself from laughing. In the end he finally asked me what music I like. 'Industrial,' I say.

He looks blankly at me.

'You know, Rammstein, Marilyn Manson, Nine Inch Nails.'

Another blank stare.

'Okay, Motley Crue?'

Blank stare.

'Don't tell me you've never heard of Tommy Lee?'

'Nope.'

Conversation dies.

My brain was thinking of ways in which I could politely excuse myself but for some reason I didn't want to be cruel to the guy and run away, especially after he offered to buy me a drink. 'Vodka and orange,' I said. 'And make it a double.' Cheeky but I needed something to numb my brain cells.

So he returned with the drink and I drunk it. 'I heard the new Son of Dork track the other day,' I said.

'They're crap,' he replied. Wow, progress.

'Yeah, they're being marketed at the next Blink182.'

'Who?'

A sinking feeling. 'Don't tell me you've never heard of Blink182?'

'Never.'

'Serious?'

He was, I really needed to escape. I put my half finished glass onto the table and announced I needed to go for a piss. I got up and walked out of the pub. I've never walked out on anyone before without saying I'm leaving, I rarely ever need to do it, but this guy was so fucking dull. By the time I'd crossed the road and was on my way home, I'd forgotten any slight twinges of guilt I might have felt about leaving him sat there.

I think that really is a bad point, well okay I don't

really, but I shouldn't be so obvious in my disdain for people. I used to be so good at feigning interest but now I simply can't be bothered, it's such a pointless waste of my energy. Why should I spend my precious moments upon this Earth with people I couldn't give a fuck about? It bores me. Lock me away in a place by myself and I'll be satisfied. That's a lie.

I'm tired of being lonely, tired of waking each day without looking forward to seeing someone. This loneliness can't be healed by surrounding myself with groups of people, it's got to be people who care about me, who would run to my side and support me when I need it. I want to be at least someone's priority. Is that so much to ask for?

Swallow a pill. Diazepam calm, makes you feel better. Numbs the loneliness that I'm not ready to deal with. It keeps the figure in the shadows away; I've seen him again. He's still waiting in the darkness for me. He can fucking wait until I'm ready for him.

Conversation with mother.

'Have any friend's over this weekend?'

'Nah, Judas was working.'

'So you don't have anyone else who normally comes round?'

'No. Judas' the only mate who comes round on a frequent basis.'

'So you haven't got a new... partner?'

'No mum, I'm still single, and no I'm not looking.'

'Ok, maybe someone will come along.'

'So how's my dog?'

'She's fine.'

I think she got the hint.

14 November 2005

'Ah shit' is all I can say; I'm bored at home with nothing to do. Great isn't it? No. I know it's stupid but I still don't feel complete, it still feels as though something is missing. Stupid after the time I've been single. Can't explain it as I've never felt this hollowness before. It feels as though something isn't there anymore. Not even the studio can fill it; guitars simply don't get out my anger, my emptiness. Build it up; the moment will come when it is due to be released.

On a lighter note, we've been recording the guitars; as usual I can't fault Judas. He's walked in and played as he was meant to. I'm happy in this at least, the one thing that is going to plan.

It's going to be weird being single at Christmas, but I'll get over it I'm sure. Whilst out walking today I walked past Lenin.

016

dirt

Then I broke. Shattered, lost and alone. Sat in silence the words spread across the page like blood, pure raw thoughts captured as they ran through my head. The cracks have grown too wide; there is no way of papering over them. My soul lays bare and this is what it sees. Honesty written on a page in front of its eyes. I am nothing. Nothing but worthless dirt.

I've convinced myself of that over the years, been treated like shit so many times that my trust has gone; fuck, at the moment I can't even trust myself. If I'm so disposable, if I can be forgotten and dismissed so easily, then I really must be worth nothing. Usable, say you like me just to get a fuck, complement me to get what you want. I'm tired, so tired of believing in something, someone, only to have it snatched out of my hand without care. How many people share a thought of me? Who thinks about me randomly and without prompting? I find it hard to believe that anyone outside my family does so. Who in their right mind would waste their time? I'm nothing, I'm dirt.

Tell me why I do this; keep carrying on putting up with this shit. I could sit here and say it's because of those I love, my mother, my brother, in part that is true but the real reason is because I'm scared what awaits me on the other side. If I knew for definite that things will be perfect, peaceful and free from pain, then I would have rotted to mud years ago. I'm scared that the next world is a place of torment, forced to re-live your worst moments for eternity, forever in pain and with no way to escape. So typically human, scared of the darkness, of the nothingness that surrounds our mortal coil. Scared of the emptiness from which we were all born.

I feel like I'm dying. My personality wasting away behind a mask. Such a happy boy, running around all the time. It's amazing how easy it is to convince people. Behind closed doors, away from the crowds these fucking thoughts of suicide kill who I am. How could that God I spent my childhood believing in have let this happen to me? What did I do that was so bad that I deserved this? So many questions, so few answers. Is anybody listening?

I've seen that figure in the shadows. That tall shadow, gaunt, the tendrils of blackness stretching out from its feet, rushing towards me. The figure in the mirror standing in corners waiting to consume me. Our silent follower, born from the same shared womb, bitter and angry that its birth went unnoticed because everyone was so concerned with us. He walks beside us; waiting for that day he will consume and steal our presence. Our death his moment of acknowledgement. I've seen him and now I'm haunted by his image. Darkness my old friend. How long will you have to wait?

Then I think there must be a reason why I am here. My redemption a distant dream that I am here to make a change, to receive a glorious payment for all this hurt, that one day everything will be alright. It's a dream I cling on to, one everyone wants to tear from my hands. But what if the future betrays me like the past abandoned me? If only we all had more time. More time to plan and pray. Why does nothing ever go my way?

I hate feeling so shit, wallowing in this self-pity. I fucking hate it when people tell you to sort it out, they don't give a fuck about you, they just don't want you to burden them, to take the limelight away from their petty 'oh-so-worrying' problems. I apologise for having a breakdown, please find it in your hearts to forgive me. I'll just sit in the corner so all those who hate me can cast their pathetic glares and where my friends will forget my existence and I can be alone to sort out my fucking head.

I don't want to die; I just want the pain to stop. It's

horrible being alone, I could just vanish tomorrow and no one would notice, I wouldn't ruin anyone's day. I could slit my wrists or overdose. Lay cold and undiscovered for days. But I don't want to die alone.

Fuck this, fuck this all. Give me a mirror, a card, I'll cut a line. How fucking vain we are; us druggies, watching our reflections as we snort. We could be so pretty if our hearts weren't broken and our souls not shattered. You feel so fucking great. I'm a fucking rockstar, why should I give a shit if people hate me? I'm only being myself. I'm nothing, I'm dirt.

Another line and I don't care; my defences are back in place. Sit up straight and tidy up. There's one stupid fucking teardrop on the mirror.

what to do with a guy who hates himself

We're walking home from the studio. We've just spent the last four hours recording more guitar parts. It's all going so well. I woke up today with a massive headache; a breakfast line cleared that. I took a diazepam pill to calm the high before getting ready to go to the studio. I've decided I need to tell someone, Judas knows I've done speed at least once in the past months, he said it surprised him as he didn't know I was into it, not that it changed anything between us, it just kinda goes to show you can know someone for years and still not know everything. But yes, I've decided I'm gong to tell him what's going on. I need to tell someone, make that first step towards salvation. It's just working out how I'm gonna word it.

'You're a bit quiet today dude,' he says.

'Yeah, just got some shit on my mind, you know kinda having one of those random days.'

He laughs, then he slows down. 'Dude, I need to ask you something. You don't need to answer.'

'Go for it.'

'I heard you talking to Bunny the other day about speed. You're not getting back into it are you?'

I pause. When he found out, I'd told him about my past using, addiction would be the word, the stories of an eighteen year old living on his own and fucking around. I'd been clean from speed for around three years until now, then well, yes, guess what happened. So how do you word the answer? 'Erm, well, I've taken a bit.'

'So is that a "yes" then? I mean it's not a problem but you know I need to know.'

Right, time to do this. 'I'm just fucking up at the

minute, having one of my down moments and it's helping. I'm sure I'll be okay in a few weeks then it'll be back to normal.' Well I don't actually know how far I'm gonna fall down this rabbit hole but I'm not going to mention that.

'Just as long as you don't go back to your old habit dude. You know I'm here for you if you need to clear some shit out your head.'

I wanna cry, breakdown on the spot and bleed my soul dry but I hold back. 'Cheers dude. I'm okay, dealing with it. But can you promise me one thing, if this shit really starts effecting my work, the album, then please beat some sense back into me.'

'No problem dude, I'll make sure it doesn't get that far.'

'I mean it dude. Physically punch the sense back. Not many people get permission to hit me.'

He laughs. 'Like I said dude. If it gets to that point I'll sort it.'

I smile. 'Thanks.' I feel somewhat lighter, a burden lifted from my shoulders. Someone knows, my mate watching out for me, he'd already been watching. True friendship. Dom and Judas, been through so much together, always looking out for each other. My mate, my guitarist and at the current moment my guardian angel.

Memory.

Rip. Roll. Snap. Rub. Slip. Slide. Grab. Pull. Don't forget to breathe. Deeper. Quicker. Heart pounding. Climax. Cum. Relief. Pull out. Fall forward. Kiss. Hug. Done.

Same pattern every time. Fuck then get fucked. Go home off my face. It was simple, fun, easy. Having sex for drugs, no great inconvenience. Get the bus home without a word. Sit in silence, fidgeting at the back. Miss the stop or get on the wrong bus and then try to find your way home. It became a routine. I knew I had to stop but why should I want to? It was free, I wasn't wasting money.

I'd   lie awake at night trying to coax myself to sleep. When time would seem to go slowly I'd put on music to make sure it passed at its correct pace. Come down. Relax. Laugh about what I'd just done or rather hadn't done. Live a whole evening and have nothing to show for it but a headache and aching muscles. Feel worn down and drained. I'd sit on the steps outside college smoking a cigarette held in trembling hands. Fun reduced to this. I had to stop. Well, at least slow down.

I awoke one day and looked at myself in the mirror. I liked who I was, hated what I did. An eighteen year old with an infatuation for a twenty five year old who fed him speed for a fuck. Nice one Dom. New low. Sort yourself out. So I did, before I could think or rethink I phoned him up and told him I couldn't do it, hung up before he replied. Detox had begun.

I buried myself in my work, engrossed myself in a band I hated. If I kept myself occupied I'd get there…

Sleepless nights. Troubled nights. Dreams of random words running through my head, conversations with friends and vivid explanations of why I needed to get fucked. I'd wake up having already thought myself awake and have to sit and think if I'd made the phone calls I'd just spent the last hour making in my head. Just ignore it all and carry on as normal, or at least work out what normal was.

I would stare blankly at a television for ages, chain smoking my way through a pack of Marlboro Lights. I'm not addicted to the feeling, I just prefer it. Pick up the phone, dial the number. Fuck. Climax. Cum. Done. Small relapses, but that was to be expected right? No. I made the final step and deleted his number.

Clean. Happy. Learn to live life as normal and be satisfied with what you've got naturally. See you can have fun, it might not be totally fucked and chemically enhanced but that doesn't make it any less enjoyable.

One last time though. Turn up. Slip. Slide. Fuck. Climax. Cum. Done…

That was four years ago. Things were different back then, I still had some belief in my own self worth. Now I am nothing. I paid for my drugs, there is no fucking. I cut and snort, pop and swallow. When I look in the mirror I hate who I am, don't give a fuck what I'm doing. I'm dirt.

Reality is so much nicer when you're on the other side of the door.

Okay, maybe I should of told Judas the true extent but how do you word it? What a burden to breakdown on your best mate. To fall from grace in front of their eyes. Surely that must be an experience, the most depressing thing in your life and at the same time the most liberating. How pathetic that I can't ask my best friend for his total help because I'm so used to people throwing my trust back in my face. You never know what people think of you until you truly need them and I'm scared to find out. What would you do with a guy who ain't happy with himself?

I have no clue myself. All I want is someone to be happy with, to laugh with, dance with. Run around holding hands and fall in love with. Someone to kiss and roll around with all day on the floor without caring about anyone or anything else. But I have no one to give me that. I have friends that care but not that one person I can love. You can surround yourself with a million people yet still be so alone. So what do you do with a man who ain't happy with himself?

You cut a line of ketamine and pretend that every fucking thing will be okay. This soul is bleeding, mourning, trying to find something to fill its aborted half and I haven't given it any time to do this. Numbed myself and carried on. Let it grow like a cancer and now the only thing keeping me going is an album that I chip away at each day. Such a lonely existence but fuck it's going to be one hell of a statement.

I'm laughing; I've just had a thought. In the past I've dated some fucked up people, well actually I worded that wrong, it should say I've broke up in some fucked up ways. I just hope the next person I date doesn't run off in obsession over their sister's boyfriend, dump me in New York, threaten me with their suicide or decide that they're straight as they run off with their hypochondriac brain tumour in tow.

24 November 2005, Thursday

So here we are two months into the recording and this is what will be the last studio session Judas and I will have this year. It's good. We've recorded some guitar parts and I've just finished the vocal take for 'Dirt'. I did it in one take, beginning to end without stopping. I let the emotions flow, released some of what I'm feeling out into the track. I know recording the vocals is going to help clear my head a bit. Hopefully.

I'm not sure, as we sit here having a break before we pack away, if I'm still keeping to my deadlines but fuck those. This album is going to get made, I can feel that more strongly with each passing moment I work on it. This is my baby, I will give it life and watch it grow. It's going to be a journey I can see that. One bit of happiness, one bit of dedication in my life.

30 November 2005

Mark just sent through the most beautiful demo I've ever heard. It stunned me to silence as I heard it. I sat there with it playing before jumping up and putting it into *Logic* and making a basic rough version. Played a loop, settled back down and picked up a pen and notebook. Words flowed so quickly. Memories hammering back into my consciousness. My conversations with God. My demons still haunting my head.

13 November 2000

I'm crying, I don't know why. Something inside me just snapped. Tears, warm salty tears roll down my cheeks. I'm trapped, maybe that's why I'm crying. Trapped in a world that has been created around me. A metaphorical prison where the walls have grown taller and taller and before I finally realised what's happening; the daylight is too far away to grasp. Sat in a shadow of pain, there is nothing I can do but sit here rocking back and forward, the tears pouring like rain onto the cell floor.

I am dirt. I am nothing. Nothing remains of me, only the husk of what I've become. Anger, hurt, hatred burn behind my eyes. There is no one I can talk to, no one who will help me. I need to run but where to? These demons will just follow. I'm numb. Why can't anyone hear my cries, my screams for help?

Alone in my room I stare at my mirror. What do I see? It's not me, I don't look like that. The vision blurs, I don't have a shape. I am no one. I am dirt. I am the unloved toy discarded without care. How can something so worthless have a shape?

I close my eyes with my hands and pray the image will go away, but when I remove them, the bloodshot eyes still stare back at me over tear stained cheeks. That isn't me. How could *that* be me? The first slice. No pain. The tears well up in the reflection's eyes. The second slice. No pain. The reflection stares hard, unblinking, tears rolling down its cheeks. I hear God turn his back. Slice. Slice. Slice. Why can't I feel pain? Why is there no fucking pain? The angel Gabriel closes his eyes. I feel empty. I need to feel pain to show me I am here, but there is nothing. In Heaven the son Christ turns up his TV. I am nothing. I am dirt.

The figure in the mirror continues to cry. The tears rolling down its face one after the other. It mouths the words 'useless, worthless, dirt' at me. I cut deeper, the chest of the image bleeding out of the slits I've made. Why won't it die? Why won't it just curl up and die?

The figure brings its hands to the side of its head. I feel mine do the same. The scalpel slips from my fingers and I fall forward, following it to the floor. Realisation, blessed realisation. It was me, the reflection had been me. I feel pain for the first time. Naked I curl into a foetal ball, hug my knees tightly. I'm still crying, as the pain increases I hug myself tighter. I am dirt. I am no one. How can I feel pain? The blood from my cut chest trickles down my side. I am no one. I am dirt.

I'm still curled in that position when I awake the next morning. I look in the mirror as I stand. Thirty odd red raw cuts across my front, a road map of pain from my collarbone to my groin. Tears sting as they fall against the wounds.

Why had I been reduced to this? Had I asked to be treated like a piece of shit? All I want is to be accepted for who I am? Why will no one accept the blame? I was told it was all my fault. Like always it was all my fault. I am to blame for wanting to ease my pain; I am to blame for all my loneliness. I'm lost. Lost within myself. There is nothing left but pain. Un-healing pain.

So I find myself again topless and alone in front of the mirror. I look at what's become of me. The figure in the mirror is me, of that I'm now certain. The cuts across its glass chest mirror those across my own. What has happened to me? What has happened to my confidence? I'm worn out, tired. Dead. A shadow of what I used to be. I'd been reduced to this. Everything has gone. Stripped away. I'm alone. No one to ease away my pain, no one to answer my screams. I despise what I see, what I've become. I look like a no one. I look like dirt.

It's time for a fresh start. The future is mine. No one is going to take it from me. Time to rise from the ashes...

That was five years ago and here I am, exactly the same. Built myself up only to be in the same position. Burning myself into the ashes. Five years of collected pain. A different room, a different mirror, the same demons clawing at my back. Here I am praying, screaming for God to listen to me, to answer me, but as always He's not looking my way. My cries not worthy of divine attention.

So many times I've called out for Him when I needed a miracle to save me. When I was stood cutting myself, did He care? No. When I was lying pinned down on my back and raped by someone that once meant so much, did He stop to help? Fuck no; *He* just let that moment kill part of me. And now, as I sit here what do I expect He will do? Absolutely fucking nothing. I just want Him to know that despite it all I'm still here, I got through without His help. Maybe I am so bad, so wrong, so evil that He believes I deserve this, but there's one thing I want Him to understand. I can see the small glimmer of hope in the distance. I've dreamt my destiny and I know I'll rise from the flames stronger, more powerful, more determined.

I hope you're listening now; I just want you to know that I'm going to be the weed that strangles the corn.

2005
DECEMBER

019

C₁₃H₁₆NClO

Stumble out of bed in the morning, force down a breakfast, write, mix, cut and paste. Fall asleep and wake up the next morning to start all over again. So much work but the volume stays the same. Day after day working on the same tracks. Routine, a creative numb.

When I finished my stupid amounts of written work and marketing plans, guess how I celebrated. I pulled out my copy of LaVey's *Satanic Witch* and made a ketamine pentagram across its cover image. Patience was a virtue but the rewards were great. My nod to someone that inspired me when I was younger. Anton fucking LaVey, how sweet your book did taste.

Glory be to the Father, and to the Son, and to the little piggy that cried all the way home.

I'm being stalked by the number 23. Every time I look at the clock it's twenty three minutes past the hour, the page in a book is a twenty three, a bus number, the amount of change I'm given. I pay for a bill on my coke dusted card, £9.23 once they add the extra 50p for tobacco sales. Fuck, even Judas witnessed the moment I finished the book on Chapter 23, page 223 at 23:23. It's haunting me and I can't escape it. How the hell can it be twenty fucking three minutes whenever I look at the time? It's become a joke, I laugh in frustration. My watch alarm still goes of at 6pm, but because the battery's dying it perceives 18:00 to be, you guessed it 22:23. The number has no significance, well actually the only one I can think of is that it will be my age when I finish this album, it also happens to be the day of the month my birthday falls on. Thinking about it I was born in February 1983, 02/1983. $(0+2)+(1+9+8+3) =$

(2)+(21) = 23... *Fuck.*

There are twenty three letters in the Latin alphabet, the twenty third letter in the English alphabet is W which is formed by two points down, three points up. Human sex cells have 23 chromosomes, and the Earth has an axial tilt of 23.5 degrees. According to the *Principia Discordia*, 23 is the sacred number of Eris, the goddess of discord. *The Lord is my Shepherd I shall not want. He makes me lie down in green pastures; he leads me beside still waters; he restores my soul... Even though I walk through the valley of the shadow of death I will fear no evil.* Psalm 23.

So I've shovelled a load of ketamine up my nose and here I am sat in my room talking to the figure, shadow, whatever peering in at me through the mirror. Apparently I have a tear in my eye but I think he's telling lies. All the clocks have paused at 23 so I've lost time, not that it's a great loss; all it ever does is tick away. Each passing second lost in eternity, never to be experienced again. All that remains are fragile crystal memories in your head.

'And what about you mirror shadow, what must your memories be like? So many moments forced upon your glassy portal, memories captured like Satan's soul reflected in the lake as he shattered upon the Earth. Visions stored and played out in alternative realms where the time runs backwards and is unseen safe for fleeting glimpses and prolonged vanities. How many faces have stared upon you to view their perceived imperfections, so much disgust poured into your world, little surprise that it's darker on your side of the mirror.'

The shadow just smiles, a brief silence before he answers. 'Your order is wrong. Remember we show you the images you see. Without us you would not see yourself as often as you do. We feed off your insecurities, we force your imperfections upon you daily, your brain sees what it wants to and we give it shape. Your disgust feeds our darkened world; the tears that fall because of us fill our oceans and rain down gloriously upon our land. When you gaze upon your reflection think of it as the sea. So much life existing beyond what is visible. Through your eyes we can see directly into your soul, yet you can't see into ours. Such a selfish world you live in when all you can think about when you see your reflection is yourself.'

'But do you have any idea how it feels to hate the reflection, to be disgusted by your own image? You simply look into our world like a window, do you see reflections or simply fuel for your darkness?'

'We see you struggle in a world so tied to a notion of beauty. What does it matter how you feel about the way you look when there is someone out there who loves it? Would you deny love for personal vanity? Such a lonely existence to live by the mirror's vision. It's a matter of perception. The ugliest duckling could look into the glass and see a beautiful swan, but then a peacock could gaze upon its reflection and see nothing but a turkey. As I said, we give shape to what you want to see, we lie. You have the power to change that but our darkness will always be there waiting to feed.

'Remember, when you gaze upon our glass what you see reflected back is not the same person everyone else sees.'

the redundant wake-up call

So here we are sat in the pub. Shelby and I, as well as the rest of our recording group for a project we've just spent the last four hours mixing. I'm happy with what we've done, it sounds fucking awesome, it was an excellent final session and we got everything done that we needed to. The best way to celebrate is to have a few drinks and relax. A few hours later and we're still going.

'You know Devon hates you,' Shelby says out of the blue. Devon a girl, not the town.

'Really? How the fuck can she hate someone she's never taken the time to talk to?'

'She was telling us the other day. She hates you because she thinks you're a fascist.'

I burst out laughing, almost spilling the drink I was bringing to my lips. How the fuck did she come to that conclusion? Now, why is it that people always jump to that conclusion about me? Do I ooze an aura of fascism? Do I have the appearance of Hitler? Yes, Dom oozes the fascist fear, the entire history of the Third Reich and Mussolini's Italy run combined through my veins. Yeah, right, whatever.

Before I can respond some random strangers join the table and take over the conversation. Speaking an endless line of bullshit to which Shelby is replying. *Oh, you've got porn on your phone, will I let you Bluetooth it to mine? No, fuck off.* They just go on and on, minutes turn into their tens and then eventually they decide to get up and leave. We've sent them on to an 'amazing' pub down the road. It's a gay bar. Shelby turns to me with a smile.

'How the fuck could you talk to such pond life?' I say.

Shelby doesn't reply, we just burst out laughing and the night continues.

I've agreed to buy three and a half grams of coke from him in the New Year.

It's 9 in the morning, the date is the ninth day of December, before me is my wallet and my head feels numb. There's a problem, a pretty major fucking problem. My wallet is empty, totally devoid of all cards and plastic. Shit, fuck, where the hell has it all gone? Breathe, think, concentrate. Try to remember the blur of the night before. I'm sure I gave them to Judas, dear God tell me I gave them to Judas and not a random stranger. I grab my phone and call the number. Judas answers.

'Dude,' I say. 'Please tell me you have all my cards.'

'I got them all.' He doesn't sound impressed.

'Bit of a mad night last night wasn't it?'

A pause. 'Yeah, you got a bit fucked.'

He had to carry me home, that much I know. 'Sorry about that dude. I didn't slam the door in your face did I?'

'Nah, I only walked you home. Don't worry about it, I mean how many times have you had to do that to me?'

I laugh. 'Any chance of getting my cards back today? I kinda need them.'

'Yeah, I'll be in Guildford later.' A pause. 'Dude we gotta have that talk.'

I know exactly what talk he means. Shit, fuck. Has it got that far? 'Okay dude, see you later.' Put the phone down and look in the mirror. Fuck, I look like crap. Go eat some breakfast, drink a sweet cup of tea then crawl into the shower to try and at least make myself look presentable. I can see my reflection as the water rushes over me. I still look like shit.

I let my mind wander back over the night; it's just a big old blur of nothing. A few nondescript faces and moments and then a big inward groan. I slap my hand against my head at the memory. Turning around in the pub toilets to see Judas just standing there in silence as I wipe my nose. His hand coming out and ripping the card from my hand. Telling me to clear my wallet of all plastic and place it in his awaiting palm. 'This is my punch in the face dude,' he says as the cards enter his wallet and he drags me from the toilet.

The walk of shame. Him dragging me out in front of all our friends and associates. All eyes upon me as he commands me to sit in a corner and slams my pint in front of me. I try to reach for it but it's always too far away and I look like a twat waving at a mirage. With no answers coming from me, everyone turns to Judas.

'He's off his fucking tits,' he says as he sits down. 'Off his fucking tits on speed.'

Punch. Public announcement of Dom's problem, his habit. Paraded in front of twenty three faces and having their disapproving glares look at you. Sit in silence. This is what salvation feels like. Humiliation after the fall. I tried not to smile about what was happening, tried so hard not to look amused about the situation. If I had any pride left it vanished in that moment.

Back in the shower I groan again, turn off the water and step out. Time to face the music. Time to attempt to look contrite. Time to go meet Judas.

I stand waiting for Judas, my head still heavy. I feel like shit, I can't be doing with people talking to me today, I think I've blanked a few people but I don't fucking care.

I see Judas, I step towards him, I see the other two mates. Shit. I nod my 'hello' and Judas pulls out his wallet, luckily he's in a rush. He hands me the cards. 'You're eyes still look pretty fucked dude,' he says.

'Bit like I feel,' I reply in a mumble.

One of the friends speaks, he left early last night. 'Why does Judas have all your cards?'

I make to answer but Judas cuts over me. 'To prevent him from cutting a line when he got home last night. He was totally fucked on speed.' He looks at me. 'Dude, look what you did.' He raises his sleeve and shows me the cuts my fingernails made when I grabbed him.

'Shit dude,' is all I can say.

'We'll talk later dude, I gotta run.'

'Okay.' We say our goodbyes and I stagger back home. Am I looking forward to the talk? Erm nope.

How the fuck could I have been fucked off my head on speed and not remember actually doing any? It doesn't make any sense, but I was caught red handed. My brain wants to say something, I let it. 'You've let it go too far,' it says.

'Fuck you,' my reply. I know it's right, kinda.

I stop at the park on the way home and sit by a tree. I try to remember, pull out some recollection of what happened. Nothing, so I just sit and let my mind empty. Momentary relaxation before BANG!

Flashback.

We're walking down the street, or rather I'm stumbling and Judas is just pulling me along and then I hear it. A ping of metal hitting the floor, my thumb rubs the now empty finger. *Shit, fuck, shit.* I stop and look, scanning with my eyes.

'What's wrong,' Judas asks.

'My ring. I've dropped my ring.'

He looks. 'We're not gonna be able to find it, it's too dark.'

'No, you don't understand, I can't lose that ring.' It means too much. A connection to a person, a memory. The One Ring which will lead me back one day.

'Dude, it's too dark.' He looks around. 'There's no way we'll find it.'

I stare at him, I want to cry. 'Oh no?' I flick my finger out without looking. 'It's right there.'

'Whatever Dom,' he says. He looks where my finger is pointing. 'What the fuck?'

I follow my finger's glare. The ring is lying exactly where it's pointing. Without care I lunge for it, feeling Judas grab and pull me back quickly. Feeling the breeze from the car that drove past. Hearing the sound of the wheels going over the ring.

'Dude, it's not important enough to die for.'

'Trust me it is.' I lunge for the ring again. Judas holds me firmly.

'You wait there, I'll grab it.' He walks away and locates the ring. He returns and puts it in his pocket.

'Dude, the ring.'

'I'll give it you when we get back to yours.'

'Just give me the fucking ring.' The words blast angrily from my mouth.

A bit shocked, Judas hands the ring over. I take it and push it home on my finger. Calm rushes over me, blessed calm. I'd die if I ever lost the ring so carelessly. I'd never forgive myself. Some things you can never replace. They mean so much more than their physical appearance.

I smile at Judas. We continue the way home, my moment of sobriety vanished and I start mumbling incoherent crap again.

I let myself smile as I open my front door. Maybe it's good that I can't remember much of that night. The important memories have lodged and that's the main thing, the important thing, everything else is redundant.

Have I truly learnt anything from this? Probably. Maybe I have been screwing myself over for no good reason, maybe it has gone too far, maybe I should take a fucking break. 'Maybe' isn't a definite so I guess it can wait. If all that humiliation and almost loss of something precious was a wake up call then it's gotten lost somewhere with the line that's just gone up my nose. There goes all the guilt with the second.

prayers for silence

Friday, 16 December 2005

So here I am, sat on the train waiting to go to Preston. The great Christmas getaway. Hopefully being away from all this shit and surrounded by my family should do the trick of kicking my ass back into gear. Fifteen weeks have passed and all I have to show for my efforts is one completed instrumental track and two fucking demos. Is that all I have achieved. I've been slaving away and that's all I've got to show for it? Granted I started late September and finished the studio in November, but I must really be falling behind. Come January it'll really kick in. I hope. No, this album *will* get made, no question about it, that is fated in the stars, part of my destined life plan. I'm trying to put my efforts down. I've worked as hard as I can based on what was available to me. You can't expect any more than that.

Fifteen weeks, however, remains a long period of time. How many lines is that? How many pills, cigarettes and glasses filled with glorious alcohol? On average I've been smoking twelve cigarettes a day, that's eighty-four a week, that's an average of one thousand, two hundred and sixty times my lungs have bled. One thousand, two hundred and sixty times my lungs have shared the air with Death, his creeping fingers gripping around and burning them with his touch. At least stuck this train they'll be granted three hours respite. If only my mind could receive that.

Constantly thinking, decrying, putting down. When you live with your demons you fight constantly. To be at peace with yourself is like sitting in front of a moonlit sea and hearing nothing but its gentle lapping against the earth at your feet, that is a peace to which I dream I could have. Instead I'm faced with a brain like a rotten sailboat wrestling with a tumultuous ocean. A solitary figure struggling to find his way through the Hellish plane of life.

It's amazing how much of my life I've spent alone. Ignored, forgotten or sometimes self induced, the loneliness that surrounds my existence gets to me; it sits at the core and eats away. In a world filled with self centred liars and two faced cretins, how the hell are you expected to trust? Trust leads to the inevitable curse of disappointment. A curse that I know all too well, so rarely do people live up to my perception of them. There's only two people I trust above all else. That's Judas and Mark, my best friends who mean the world to me.

I just had a thought, to go randomly off subject, but it's amusing how people of different professions all have different characteristics. I mean I know it's not rocket science to understand why but I've never taken the time to notice. For example, let's look at a few people I've met in the past year:

The music producer - usually believes totally in their own self worth; fucking bitchy as hell.

The fashion designer - always appears to be sizing you up as if trying to imagine you in some item of clothing they are designing.

The aged 'rockstar' - likes to deny their age and go for kids at least two decades younger than themselves.

The actor - like their roles on stage their character is constantly changing. You never know who they really are and I bet they don't either. Hard to trust because they believe that they are such good liars when in fact they're transparent as fuck.

The train's moving, everything just a blur outside the window. Strange to think when I made this same journey last year, I was sat next to someone I loved, had conversations with a deaf woman, concocted some terrorist life for a random stranger and was delayed due to someone throwing themselves in front of a previous train. Makes this solitary journey even more depressing. It snowed on Christmas day last year; I doubt it will again on this one.

My bedroom is exactly the way it was when I last left it, the way it always is, the way it looked when my eyes gazed upon it at eighteen. I dump my bag and look around. I can see things that bring back memories of when I last slept here. Then I wasn't alone. On the bedside table is an empty pack of Sam's Marlboro Lights; even a few butts lie in the ashtray. On the floor by my feet, a t-shirt he'd forgotten to pick up and take with him. I grab it; it still smells of him. This is *my* room, I lived in it before I even knew of his existence and yet somehow it's like he's taken control of it, littering it with memories of him. This time last year I was happy, now I'm just, well, I don't know what the fuck I am. I just exist with a task to complete. So many memories locked within this one room.

If you stand in silence for a while and let the distant noises roll into your ears, you realise how small and insignificant you are, such a lonely world when you stand by yourself. All those people you know, knew, hated or loved are all co-existing at the same time, all of them not sharing you a single thought, for the moments you are not around, you do not even exist. I often think and wonder if there's anyone thinking about me at that given time. Do I mean so much to someone that they sit and wonder about me? How beautifully saddening for two people to be thinking about each other at the precise same moment and wonder if the other still thinks about them.

Each and every day since we said our goodbyes, I think about Sam, I can't help it. Habit I guess, I doubt he does the same, by this point I'd be consigned to a distant memory. Fuck, why does he still get to me? I don't think about any of my other lost connections at all and yet I can't let him join them. What does that say about me? What he means to me? I feel like I'm in some pathetic limbo waiting for a day when everything sorts itself out and he returns to my side. Who am I kidding? I just need something to heal these scars, something to make me numb. I could self medicate myself with whatever shit I can stick up my nose but the reality will never change, it'll always be there waiting for me. I simply don't want to live in this pain anymore.

If I go to record I know his voice is on the multi-track, attempting to sing one of RDI's songs. One we'll record again around his track. So hard to delete that ghost of a memory. I feel so empty inside, so used and discarded. Everything I felt for him seems so pathetically meaningless, but I guess that's how it has to be.

This isn't a holiday; I've still got work to do. I can't let this album fall behind. Mark's going to be doing his first parts for this project. We'll be recording a series of acoustic tracks, just pure acoustic guitar and vocals. I plan for them to represent the opposite side of the album proper; they'll be the calm, intimate underbelly. The acoustic heart to the chaotic body.

Wow, I finally managed to wear myself down, I just fell asleep at the computer whilst editing up everything. I've been working full steam on this for so long it's like I haven't allowed myself a break. I'm tired and yet there seems to be so little to show for it. I know it's just gonna suddenly all come together and I'll be like 'wow' but it's just getting to that point. I just hope everyone likes the finished product at the end.

I've been trying to think of how I'd sum up 2005. Well, all things considered, it was a good year. I mean it started good, had a good middle and a good end. It was a very musical year, I counted up how many tracks I've done and it came to something like thirty plus. *And* I went to see Motley Crue.

I love it when I can say that a year has finished with no regrets. Everything seems to have worked out for the best. A lot happened but I've learnt one thing this year. The present looks to the future not the past.

The one thing that 2005 confirmed for me was my

belief that the word 'love' is a simple four letter word that people can say with ease and without meaning. I'm just content in the knowledge that every time I said it this year I meant it, and never stopped meaning it.

At the end of the year, two things remain the same. My watch alarms are always set at 6pm, and I still wear a solitary ring on my finger.

Hey, look everyone; Dom's trying to appear positive. Seems out of place doesn't it?

I can't breathe, I can't see, I can't be anything but me. All of this anger, why won't it fade? Is this why I have been made?

Mark always surprises me when we record. I mean not in the sense that he can play, but in the fact he doesn't realise how good he is. He'll play it through then insist on re-recording it even though there's absolutely no need. I guess he's just a perfectionist like myself. This is his moment to shine on the record and he wants it to be awesome, and listening back to the rough mixes that's pretty much what he's achieved.

It's New Years Eve and I'm tripping, just my final dash of coke for when I have to do my vocals. New Year's Eve and I'm working, recording some of the most emotional lyrics on this album. I've done most of them, 'In Dreams', 'Pain', 'Life', even 'Dirt' went off with no problem, but now I have to record *that* song. The dark song. To date probably my best lyrics, maybe I'll never write any as good as these in the future. '13-11-00', my conversation with God. I'm sat on the floor holding the microphone; I can feel the tears welling up again. This is one of many attempts to get this right. It has to be perfect. The record button is pressed, the backing track starts. *I hope you're listening now…*

Images flashing through my mind, sat in this same position, raw cuts across my chest, the warm trickle of blood and pain, such glorious pain. *Back then I was so scared, my prayers not good enough it seems.*

There's no break in the vocals, the monologue just rolls on, no chorus just words. A message, a statement, an ending. This will close the album. I feel a tear drop, I carry on, a slight break in the voice. Track ends. The clocks strike midnight. Happy Fucking New Year.

I listen back; it's the take we want, the perfect emotion, so dark and pitiful. Then I hear it, a voice, a different voice. A cold chill runs through me. Rewind, play and turn up the volume. It's there, no mistaking it. There's a tear in my eye for some reason at its presence. It could have almost ruined it.

I call Mark to show him, maybe he can confirm or dismiss it. His reaction is the same as mine. His face white.

Rewind, play. Two voices, one my own, the second a muffled harsh whisper.

'I hope you're listening now…'

'No.'

happy fucking new year

It's strange, only a few days into the year and already 2006 feels like a good one. All my working my ass off recording, editing and mixing has paid off. I now return with the second part of the album done. Twenty-one minutes of dark acoustic tracks dealing with subjects of depression and deceit. Five simplistically beautiful tracks to complement the main album. Mark's playing was awesome; I can't believe how much I love these tracks. It's set me up for the tasks of this year. Finish the album. It's gonna be a busy few months but I'm ready and waiting to take it on headfirst. This is the year of RDI.

I've finally decided I'm gonna clean myself up a bit. I mean those lines, pills are distracting, they made me break all my rules of recording and I don't want them to slow me down. It's funny how everything so far except Mark and Judas' guitars have been recorded under the influence of something, but that's gonna change. I took my last line on New Year's Eve and it captured an emotion. New year, new beginning. I can't afford to lose sight of the road ahead.

I actually truly feel positive about everything, like, I dunno, like I shed a few demons when I recorded '13-11-00', 'Dirt' and all the other tracks. Closed certain chapters of my mind's pain. '13-11-00' sends chills down my spine, even in its current unfinished state. It's just so dark, so personal. Everyone reads something from it. It's the definite album closer. That means I'm in such a perfect position, I've recorded the opening and closing tracks, so now I just need to fill in the middle.

I can sense something brewing. I dunno call me paranoid but I didn't get a New Year's message from Judas this year. I know that sounds stupid but since we've been mates I've always got one, regardless of how fucked he's been; it was simply missing, even Mark mentioned it. My new year was greeted with that voice, the clock chimes and the joyous cheers and booms of parties independent of my life. It's not really a new beginning as we're nowhere near the end, but could any one give a fuck about the pain of an old friend? How many lies told in that one change of a minute?

I can see all their smiling faces, I can hear all their celebrations but I've long since stopped wondering where my invitation is. I don't want to be part of their parties of lies and pathetic non-fulfilling dreams. The night passes and they step back onto the conveyor belts of their lives and let themselves be led around in muted apathy. Why lie to themselves when they have no intention of changing? Why be part of that bullshit? If you truly want to change then fucking do it, things don't happen without action.

From the moment we're born we are on a journey towards our destiny, when we stick true to that we can feel it but it is the easiest path to get disheartened on and simply stop. I'm rumbling down that path at the moment. This little section has its ending set in stone, there's no way I can deviate. I have a direction for once in my life and I intend to grab onto it.

the needle's addiction

Using 'you' as an indefinitely specified person or persons…
you make me sick.

Using 'I' as the nominative pronoun used by a speaker
in referring to himself… *I* make myself sick.

Maybe I'll explain, maybe I won't. Time will tell.

It's thirteen days into the New Year and despite the temptations
available through boredom I've remained clean. Teetotal, I
haven't even drunk a drop of alcohol. Yesterday was the first
studio session of the new year and everything is back on track.
One addiction being pushed aside for another. So far both have
coexisted and now I've got to convince myself that they can
exist separately. It's no lie, I'm addicted to music, I've said it
before and I'll say it again. All I have done this year so far is
nothing but record, edit and mix. I've been remixing and
cleaning up the recordings from Christmas and last night Judas
and I started up again on the album proper, although being the
stupid dumb-ass I am I left the CDs of material in the studio.
That is why this morning I had to get up stupidly early to go
get them before they had chance to 'disappear' and thankfully
not only were they still there, they sounded fucking awesome.

Of course all this work is making me somewhat anti-
social but this is *a* priority, my impact on music, my future, all
in all it's me and to be told that it is the best work people have
heard from you makes it all worthwhile. Yet I can't help but
feel a little guilty that at the moment my only real human
contact has been when I've gone out clubbing and fucked
some random guy just to get a release. I think that I've
forgotten how to act normally around people now I don't have

chemicals rushing through me. I'll just have to make the effort to relearn. I wouldn't normally feel too bad about sleeping with someone just for the fun, but I was, am meant to be dating this guy I met in December but I've just simply lost interest. He isn't important; I don't have time for relationships. That's partly why I make myself sick.

Anyway, the subject is addiction and I'm not addicted to guys, I have however found a new addiction, one which will definitely put a rest to that self-destructive bullshit I'd been pushing through me. Note: a) I don't think it's bullshit, and b) I lied about being clean for thirteen days *but* I am trying to be positive here, can't you tell?

So this new addiction, what is it? The tattoo needle, and at £65 per hour it's one fucking expensive addiction. There is a twofold reasoning in my head about why now is the time to get inked, firstly because I've always wanted one and I'm now comfortable in myself and body to get it done, and secondly, it's gonna help distract me from my other addictions. The money needs to be in the bank for each session, so I can either have thousands of needle pricks mark my skin forever or put some powder up my nose for a few hours. I opted for the former.

16 January, 2006 | 23:23
Why do I still miss you?

So January is just rolling on, flashing by and I am getting more social. My time is spent either in the studio, the pub with Judas or just hanging out at Trollspiel - that's the tattoo studio by the way. I'm getting comfortable communicating again and it feels good. I can now honestly say, hand on heart, I have not stuck anything up my dear little nose since the moment that tattoo needle hit my skin. I can focus clearly for once and I'm actually starting to like myself. I'm not that bad a person. I'm recovering and it feels good. Like no cares, ok, that is a lie but I don't want to think about that, at all. Period. Four months on and I haven't spoken to myself about it. I'm not ready to. I can't. It hurts too fucking much. It still makes me cry. I need to store that emotion for my vocals, then I'll deal with it. Promise... I don't make promises, except for the one on my finger. So I won't promise, I'll just endeavour to try.

I had a conversation with that dude I was dating and he said something I've been told before, constantly, it's why people don't trust me or want to get into a relationship with me. Two observations that sum me up perfectly: a) 'You're hard to read and I can usually read *anyone*'; b) 'I think it's coz you're so "straight".' And those people, are my problems.

Why would I want to be easy to read? I'm an enigma. I'll show people what I want them to see of me. I'm smiling to the world at the moment, stupid goofy grins of delight that I'm happy doing what I'm doing. The face is just a surface, like the ocean it conceals what lies beneath.

the short tale of the evil phone

Monday, 23 January 2006

I got my new phone the other day, a Motorola *RAZR V3* thing, but since then my old phone has started acting well fucking weird. Let me explain, at random parts of the early morning, at times that don't usually exist to me, it starts emitting this weird jingle, vibrates and starts flashing in such I violent way that I'm awoken from my slumber. When I finally reach it and pick it up, there is an ominous message glowing on its screen demanding that I 'insert SIM card'. I mean it's turning itself on just to command me to insert a fucking SIM card. I'm expecting to wake up tomorrow and find my nice phone ripped to shreds and hear a self satisfied beep coming from the evil phone. It's evil. Pure evil.

Tuesday, 24 January 2006

Awoken by the flashing and whirls of noise emitting from the evil black and silver phone, Brodo Ballbagins emerged from the comfort of his room into the cold and frosty landscape. His vision and mind blurred by sleep, he crawled into the evil lair of monotone where he was instantly targeted by the evil prog-king of the realm of Beboptopia who realised that this young scamp's intention to sit at the back of the lair meant he could fall asleep. Brodo managed to placate this fearsome foe but soon found that the evil king's jazz-fusion mind wank lulled him onto the world of sleep.

Awoken by the sounds of a garish noise - namely the Village People - Brodo thought he had been transported to the seventh level of Hell, but when his eyes cleared it was just the end of the prog-king's monotone. So he left the building of doom and he made to traverse back to the sanctuary of his home.

Arriving safely back at his humble home, he informed his brother that they would be leaving to go on yet another quest. They re-emerged into the Siberian winter landscape and traversed towards the lair of the War Paint Dwarf, for Brodo's need to arrange for his next appointment and extension of his permanent war paint. As they walked they encountered many sights, namely the estate of richness known only as Aragon Court, and found new and wonderful park lands that had until then lain undiscovered.

Brodo bought himself some Atomic Sourballs, but their non-sourness left him feeling disappointed and somewhat robbed… but he ate them anyway.

One day ends, another begins. It's all just an endless quest.

the melancholy

Essay

The infinite sadness of mankind is the fact that our own advances are the means to our destruction. The industrialisation of our race, the advances in our understanding of physics and chemistry, the belief in a greater good have helped us not only to live longer and in greater comfort, but also to kill, destroy and eliminate the lives and dreams of millions of others. We create the very objects that allow us to sit, tune in, zone out and ignore the deaths and pestilence we allow our governments to inflict upon the world. Blinded by celebrity we dismiss such trivial inconveniences like the deaths of a few thousand.

Mankind has a stench. It's the stench of greed, death and destruction. A cloud of melancholy raining giant drops of despair onto the desolate landscapes we cause. A race of apes blindly following maniacal leaders in their quest for world domination, offering meagre donations to charities as a way to cleanse our souls from the blood shed by the acceptance of the lies we so blindly swallow.

As you sit and worry over some starving creature in a foreign land, maybe take the time to worry about what your government is doing, after all that is more important. Get your priorities right, your pennies may help keep some unknown alive but your apathy is helping kill the lives of innocent people. Sorry that was stupid of me. How dare I even contemplate that our children's future is more important than helping people who are beyond repair.

When you finally open your eyes and turn to your god and pray, remember that he is not listening. He long since turned his back on us. What god of love and peace could sit and watch all the destruction his angst-ridden children are creating in his name? To do that he would have to be human.

But why should we care as we go about our daily existence, locked behind computer screens or teaching our youth the morals of a blind incompetent government? Why should we care as we sell goods and help bring new life into this dying world? Why should you care? I care because if at least one person stops and decides to take a stand then maybe change will be brought about. As scientists struggle to find a cure for cancer, we fail to realise that mankind is the cancer. We are the Earth's cancer. An ever-growing genetic mutation, destroying the Earth's beauty, never resting until we ruin and kill the body that spawned us.

decadent sodomiser

So far it seems this has been a rather sexless tale, if only that was the case in reality. Up to this point in the journey its mention has been irrelevant, unimportant. My love affair was with chemicals not bodily contact. So now as I'm sat here not using, clean system and mind, I have the 'pleasure' of enduring that journey back through the minefield that is my sexual life. There is a reason for all this; it isn't just a quest for personal gratification or contempt. I'm faced with the possibility of a new 'relationship' and I need to know why I'm so reluctant to commit to it or anyone for that matter.

So where do you want me to begin? Yes, I'm one of those dirty soulless queers, wasting my semen on guys' chests and up their ass. I'm gonna be burning in Hell with a pitchfork up my butt, but hey that sounds kinda fun, at least it'll be warm. I'm actually really glad that I'm gay, and if you don't like it then I advise that you skip this chapter, or if you're scared that what you might read will give your heterosexual penis bone then likewise. Skip.

I've always been honest about my sex life. Honest and open, maybe a bit too open but I don't care. It's just sex at the end of the day, the thing porn is made of. So this will be no exception, but still, where to start? The beginning is always a good start.

Virginity was lost at fifteen. It wasn't romantic, it wasn't the next step in a long loving relationship, no, as with most things in my life it was just matter of fact. She was a girl, an American dancer staying at my aunty's Bed and Breakfast on the Isle of Skye. She was there performing at the yearly games, I was there on holiday. I don't know her name; she didn't know mine. We fucked unprotected on the sofa, my mum and aunty asleep in the next room. The only record was a comment in the guestbook that my aunty scribbled out. *The guy in the Marilyn Manson shirt was cute.* I went home the next day, didn't speak to her. I could have a seven-year old kid somewhere and not know about it. Scary thought.

At fifteen I also fucked my first guy; again it wasn't romantic. He was in the year below, he was cute, he knew my name, I knew his, can't remember it though. We used to jack each other off in classrooms as my mates stood outside, unaware of our presence. Then we fucked in the toilets during lesson time. Him bent in front over the toilet one hand on the wall, the other on his dick, me inside him unprotected using spit as lube. I came inside; he shot all over the wall. We didn't clean it up. I had a cigarette after. Guess that's the point that confirmed in totality that I was gay.

They say you always remember the names of your first. I don't remember either of them. What does that say about me?

I didn't have a boyfriend until I was twenty, not because the opportunity was never there, just that it never happened. Well I kinda had one at eighteen but I'll never talk about him, I'm still not ready to. Maybe I will later, we'll see. He killed a part of me. Bastard. So yeah, first boyfriend at twenty, so that meant I missed out on being one of those cool loved-up teenage couples, settling instead for random wanks on buses, in libraries, fucking in woodlands and college classrooms. Most of them I knew their names, a few I didn't, names were sometimes irrelevant. Touch. Wank. Suck. Fuck. Cum. Done. Fuck off. Don't get an idea that I was ashamed or that I have issues with sex, I'm not and I don't, it was simply the fact that the sex was more important than the person in some cases. What kind of person does that make me?

My attitude at times was quite simple. I hated when you'd fuck someone you don't know and they'd want to talk after it. They wanted a fuck; they got what they wanted. If they'd wanted a cup of tea and a chat afterwards they should have said. I'd hate how having edged towards a door to make my escape, I would then find myself an hour later listening to them telling me their life story. I mean sorry, if you're not a friend then why would I care? Well, here's where it gets shallow - that is unless you're really good looking. I've always placed too much emphasis on beauty.

I also used to say my name was Steven sometimes.

So at twenty I decided I'd slept around enough. For near enough five years I'd rolled around with my fair share of people in beds around both the North and South of England. At eighteen I got bummed by a Head of some High School, obviously not my own, but he liked to fantasise throughout that I was a student, which freaked me out somewhat. He was shit anyway. That's not the point however; the point was I became bored. Desensitised to it all. Sex was sex, nothing more. It meant nothing more than a moment of pleasure. Justification that people found me attractive. That for that moment I was their sole concern. It filled a desire and that was it. It had to stop. It had to change. It did change. I can remember when as well. I woke up one day in an unknown bed, in an unknown house; it was even an unknown town. The guy tried it on with me when he woke up. I told him I was fifteen and if he didn't drive me home I'd call the police. He believed me.

I became hard to get. Then I met a guy called Mark. He changed things. I loved for the first time. Not true love, I know that now, but then it was everything. He showed me care, he showed me affection. He was also the hardest thing in my life. My first true boyfriend and he was HIV+. I know it's selfish but in the end that was what placed most pressure on me. At twenty I wasn't mature enough to cope. I'd try, but there were nights I'd sit awake crying that this would literally not last forever, that the person I loved was dying in front of me and there was nothing I could do to stop it or help. He dumped me in a bar in New York a month after my twenty-first birthday. He insisted on going to a gay bar that night. I ended up going home with a stranger as a rent boy, I made $300; Mark didn't come back to the hotel until 9am the next morning. We never spoke about why not; we knew we weren't in love. It was well and truly over.

A month later I met Sam. That was love. True love. The love of Shakespeare. We were together for a year and a half, the year spent together daily without break. It was intense, it was perfect. It is why I'm here, fighting with my feelings. It's been five months or so since it ended, I don't want to even think about how many people I've fucked since. For the first few months it was almost two different guys each week. The drugs put a stop to that though. I didn't need 'comfort' or 'acknowledgement'; with them I *knew* I was fucking hot. They made me feel good about myself, the way *he* used to make me feel. I've never been vain enough naturally. I'm a living contradiction. I know I'm good looking but I don't believe it. Go figure.

So here I am for the third time since Sam, being wanted by one person and still I'm lost. The first one I walked away from. The second I didn't have the courage or want to commit. The day I was gonna ask him if he wanted it to go further he walked out from the shower and collapsed on the floor. I'd laughed until I realised he'd actually fainted and smacked his head against the wall. Then I'd panicked and the moment had been lost. It never came again and he was forgotten. Small things like that amuse me.

I'm gonna think about it. Okay, this current guy, we've been on a few dates and he wants to make it serious. How do I feel? Well he annoys me; he has an obsession with Buffy and moans on to me about his ex all the fucking time. I just find myself sitting there grinning and saying 'ooh how nice,' when in fact I just want to say 'It wasn't "love" you had with your ex or I had with mine. Gay people don't feel love, that's a straight emotion.' That's something I actually believe at this moment, another contradiction. Maybe it'll change, maybe it won't. It's overrated anyway.

Piss, cunt, fucking fuckity fuckwit, bullshit, crap. My

little world is being infiltrated by a return of random phone calls and text messages. Why do I feel like I'm being sucked into a relationship? Be honest Dom, you know where this is headed. A big fat nowhere, especially since whilst 'dating' him I fucked some other guy's ass in some random back garden without care. I *don't* want to be in a relationship, I don't have time for a relationship, and I'm not getting into one just so I can feel wanted, needed, 'loved'. That would be so wrong, that would be cruel.

Single I shall stay. He'll get over me; they usually do anyway. Okay, rant over. I've still not come to terms with my last one, still haven't done the gay ass soul-searching bollocks. Until I can be bothered I'm going to find a sand pit so I can bury my head in it. It's bubbling to the surface. I can feel the eruption is brewing. *Shit*, who said love was easy? Oh yeah, gays don't feel love do they?

needle kiss

Whilst we're in the process of being all honest and open, I've got another confession to make, another secret hidden away up to this point. I guess it's all part of the procedure; to overcome you need to realise; then everything makes sense. We all know that time passes and the seasons quietly change in rotation, yet that doesn't remove the melancholy from the brain. Life is like a novel in reverse, a happy series of events with the unhappy ending.

I've tried to be honest on these pages, haven't covered up or made excuses for myself. Live without regrets I say. I mean why feel remorse about something that at the time felt right? I was gonna leave this shit hidden under the carpet or locked away but the problem with shit is that it stinks and if un-removed that stench lingers. Maybe I'm just disgusted with myself, no, not disgusted, shocked, disappointed that I did it. I knew it would happen one day but was that how far I'd gone? I'm twenty-two, just about to turn twenty-three, yes that fucking number that's haunted me for the past months, and so far I've had this on and off relationship with various substances spanning seven years. I'm young, I'm meant to experiment but to inject cocaine, surely that's like an abortion to the pain my mum went through all those years ago. Let him who fears the needle be saved from Satan's salvation.

I guess I've always had a fascination with needles, I've always had needles, syringes and blades in my room ever since I was fifteen and Mark used to bring them home from wherever he was working at that time. I used to use them to cut art into my torso, so much more precise than a blade. I have a thing for pain. Pain is pleasure. I remember walking in from school when I was sixteen and being summoned into the kitchen by my mum who pulled up my shirt to check my arms for marks. I'd stupidly left a needle and syringe in her en-suite the night before when I'd used her shower. 'I was popping spots,' I'd told her. She didn't believe me and for the next year I'd receive random spot checks of my arms, being so pale didn't help either. Maybe that's what made it so easy, it was expected of me. Mark once spoke to someone from my year in High School, I was eighteen at the time, the conversation was along the lines of. 'Yeah, my brother's called Dominic.'

'Dominic Lyne? *The* Dominic Lyne?'

'There wasn't any other one I know of.'

'Oh, what's he doing? We all thought he'd be fucked out of his head on drugs by now.'

Glad I lived up to expectations, but thanks for seeing what I couldn't see coming. Maybe I could. There's no point in maybes, they're redundant possibilities. You act, you do. Only *one* outcome.

So the now, or the then as it is. I can't remember the first time I injected coke, well I can, I just can't pinpoint its date in my head. It's a blur, a stupid blip in my mind. I looked through the photos on my computer and there's one where I look empty eyed with a nice bruise forming on my left arm, so I'm guessing it was around that time, my arrogance would have wanted a visual record for prosperity. The photo was taken on 10 November 2005.

Two things struck me when I saw the picture. The first was how empty the eyes look. Soulless and unhappy. Sad eyes and their silent screams. The eyes are portals to the soul they say; well on that day there was no one home. The second was how obvious the shadow of the bruise was. Why did no one notice it? Why did no one say anything? Did they see or choose not to? Who knows, I didn't until now but we always see things when it's too late, it's the human way.

Please don't get the impression that the needle never left my arm; that I jacked up all the time. I don't know the exact amount but it was hardly many. I guess the word 'few' could be used. A few times when I needed that instant burst. Let's just say that my tattoo will cover up more than just skin. Did I ever say that the feel of a tattoo needle pounding my skin gives me a bone?

So why am I telling you all this? Partly to clear my own mind, partly through honesty, mostly because it'll make sense of what's coming next. I'm not ashamed like I said. Shocked, disgusted slightly, remorseful *never*. Regret is a wasted feeling; it changes nothing. Life is all about learning from your past. Sometimes we never learn.

I'd hatched a scheme in my head, a little cunning plan which I didn't know would work or not but it was worth a try. As typical fate would have it, it did and that's why now I'm sat here looking at my new set of needles and syringes. Yesterday I simply walked into the G.U.M. clinic with a load of old ones and took advantage of their needle exchange service. Simple as that, that's what it's designed for after all. I don't know where the urge came from to do it, it just appeared and I didn't back down from it. This will be my birthday present to myself. I mean I've been good, I've not touched anything for a month, I deserve a treat especially given that twenty-three is such a big thing for me lately.

I've actually got a twitch at the moment, seeing it all lined up in front of me. Needle, syringe, spoon, wrap of cocaine. Is it wrong that I've actually got a bone just looking at it? I'm being good; I haven't touched any of it. Only one more day and then *Happy fucking Birthday*. For the first time in years I'm actually looking forward to it.

It's snowing, actually snowing. I awoke to a chill in the air and that glow you only get when there's snow, the glow that unleashes the inner child's desire. The landscape is dusted with white. It's not deep, it's not massively thick, but it's snow. Snow is romantic in my life; it's always there when something important on my path through this world happens. It snowed on Christmas the year I spent it with my love. Quite fitting that it should be snowing now; now that I've turned twenty-three on the twenty-third day of the month. Twenty bloody three. I watch the snow, transfixed. High, I guess I should hide the needle before I lose it. Yes, it's my birthday; before I did anything I gave myself my own present.

It's snowing on my birthday. I pull away from the window. My mum got me Tim Burton's *Corpse's Bride* on DVD and a box of mints. I'm gonna go watch that and eat the sweets, right after I've stood in the snowfall. Tim Burton created the world; I know that, I've seen it. Only fitting that I've ticked all my favourites today. It's 9am, long day ahead of me. Johnny Deep does the voice of Victor. Bonus.

Did I just anticlimax you? Sorry I didn't explain the procedure, the feel of metal entering my skin. What's the point? You've all had injections, use your imagination. If you want to know how I feel, then it's a little blank. My brain screamed at me as I did it, the cocaine silenced it but the memory of its words lingers. *What the fuck are you doing?* it shouted. *What they fuck do you think you're doing?* What the fuck have I done? I guess some highs are too good to give up on.

Fuck that! This is what I'm trying to deal with; I don't need to fuel this demon. I was doing so well, even with this tale you don't realise how well. I wanna smash my head against the brick wall, just to knock some sense into my stupid being. I can't even just sit and enjoy myself anymore, always beating myself up, always letting my demons open their stupid mouths, always listening to what they say. Why can't I simply let myself be happy?

Weak am I? Need to fuel my temptations? I just don't limit myself, but if I carry on like this will I reach my goal? Will this album get recorded if I'm eternally wasted? Maybe, but will it be the best it could be? Maybe not. Maybes are not an option. A choice needs to be made and acted on. How does it feel demons now that I've snapped all your food pipes? See all those broken needles? How does that feel? I know how it makes me feel. Liberated. Look at me, I'm a rockstar, I'm a bright star, the star you wipe clean when I'm dirty. A ruined high and a collection of broken needles my birthday present to myself. Get me.

I'll cut a line, use the rest of this coke and fuck the day to hell. It's my birthday and no one fucking cares. None of my friends have even bothered to wish me a good one or ask me out for a drink. Dickheads. I surround myself with dickheads.

Right, I'm gonna get water. At least have something healthy today. Turn, walk, trip flat onto my ass. Look at me, crippled on the floor. Then I hear it, the laugh, the faint laugh of my birthday twin. She always visits every year. I'm glad you find this so funny. I'm glad someone does. Actually come to think of it so do I. I start to laugh. This is so fucking stupid. Happy birthday Dom. You idiot.

dream sequence

23 February 2006

I'm sat in the middle of a roundabout, houses line both sides, the only light coming from them is the blue flickers of television sets through net curtains. *In those buildings are living people,* I think. *Living people with dead souls; souls ruined by the television they watch and the lies they believe.*

I look up into the night's sky and stare at the stars. I feel alone, totally alone, like I'm the only one. Surely there must be someone like me out there. I think to myself and ask God a question. 'Why? Why have you let so much happen and never stopped to help? Why do I always feel the need to move on to another place or level?'

Then I hear a voice in my head. 'God doesn't help angels, they have to help themselves. They are marked out to keep on the move, to help and guide.'

'But what of those around me?'

'If they live in darkness with dying souls then God doesn't help the dead. Show them how to achieve their dreams. If they turn their back on you then they are destined to a life of regret.'

Silence. I stand up and see my shadow, the set of wings fading from my back. The pain they cause is the burden I have to bear. I smile as I walk down the centre of the road. One day I'll be going home, but I've still got work to do.

a short rant

27 February 2006

You would have thought I'd be used to it, but it still sickens me, I hate seeing people kissing ass in front of my face. I mean who in their right mind thinks that kissing ass is a good thing? It only makes you look desperate.

People who constantly kiss ass and suck cock to get ahead make me sick, as to me they have no self-respect. They're kinda like the people who become the people they said they would never be just in order to feel popular. I have no time for these social chameleons, I want someone to be themselves, not Peter one week then Steve the next. Seriously, do they really think that they are happy? Have they convinced themselves that having someone else's cock in their mouth, or ass on their lips is making them a happier, better and more rounded person? Yeah, because you can be truly happy being someone you're not. Yeah right. No wonder so many people are on Prozac or stuffing their faces full of drugs. It's not to make them happy, it's not to make them feel more alive. It's to numb the pain that they're not being true to themselves, it blocks the fact that they've become part of the 'crowd' that used to make them feel sick. Whatever makes you feel 'happy' I guess.

I'm glad that I've never knelt in front of anyone. It hasn't happened and it's never going to happen. I just can't do it. I can't be something I'm not and I'm fucking well proud of the fact that my self respect will rather see me squatting in the gutter than selling myself out. I'm never going to sell my soul for the simple fact that it doesn't belong to anyone else but myself. I'm never going to compromise. Everything gets done my way. You'll never see me sucking cock just to get ahead. You'll never see me being anyone but myself. If you don't like that then hey, fuck off out of my face, you'll be forgotten in a few days.

In the words of Bunny: *He doesn't give a fuck who you are; he doesn't give a fuck if you know who he is or not, he doesn't give a fuck if you don't like him. He's Dom. He generally doesn't give a fuck about anything other than what is important to him. That's why he's the coolest person in this room.*

Last night RUTT played a gig. Judas was distant, the support band, which Ward also plays bass in, played a new track; it sounded like one of Judas'. Something is happening in the shadows, I can feel it.

2006
MARCH

set free - how do you feel now?

So finally it came, the outpouring, the release. My mind finally ready to deal with what's been eating away at it, corroding it like acid. Some things are easy to deal with; rejection isn't one of them.

I don't know where it all came from, it just poured out of me one morning as I sat there with a pen and paper in front of me. All the anger flooding from me, all the words I've ever wanted to say. Honesty in pen and ink.

The question I've always wanted to know the answer to. *How do you feel now?* Does he feel any regret? Any upset about the loss of what we had? How long did he deceive me? How long did he know? So many questions all pushed to the back of my mind. The last few months of mine and Sam's relationship was definitely strained, so why did I never see it coming? Maybe I did but pushed my head into the sand as usual. So many maybes used as excuses for my ignorance, the truth is I really didn't see any of it coming. It just fell out of the blue and crushed me on the spot and stupidly it still hurts.

I'd existed cocooned in a poisoned web of lies that soon snapped under the strain of all the deceit. Unravelled I fell naked to the floor alone and cold. Drained, empty, lost. You put so much effort in and it gets thrown back at you. They go back to their old lives as if nothing has happened and complain when they get used again. The tumours in their heads telling them to start living a lie to fit in, and soon the lie becomes the truth and they lose everything that you used to love about them.

So Sam, how do you feel now? Did you ever think about me? Spare me the time of day when you woke some days, alone and set free from the shackles of a relationship? All that time we spent together, did you ever miss any of it, or care about how I felt? I was bleeding inside, tried to rip out my heart to throw discarded at your feet so you could stamp on it and destroy it forever. Did you ever care about that? Did you? All this pain, this emptiness which I tried to fill with useless addictions and brain numbing substances, just for a little peace of mind. Everyday I've shared a thought for you, bet you can't say the same. But now I've woken from that dream, that haze. I don't need this cancer any more.

So how do you feel knowing that when I think of you now I just see a lost lonely child? Lost and alone, surrounded by clones and users. All your dreams dying around you simply because no one supported them, no one believes in you like I did. Live this life you've created because you were too scared to follow your dreams; never had the commitment. I saw talent, they saw waste. What does that matter now anyway?

I'm happy now; well. getting there, at least now this burden has been shed. I can see clearly for the first time in ages and I'm still following the path to my dreams. You gave me creativity and now I'm using it. So I hope you're happy, I hope that you're sky high, I hope you've got what you want. I'm glad you set me free. So how do you feel now?

a crack opens

A few hours after my mind clearance and creation of a minimal backing track, I find myself waiting for the studio knowing I'll be doing the vocals for it today whilst the emotion is fresh, that's the way it needs to be done. There is however something in the air and I don't like it. I'm stood waiting with a fag in my mouth at my usual place and Judas is nowhere to be seen. Normally he's early like me. I'm thinking too much I guess; clear minded I find myself over analysing everything. It's a little disturbing.

Judas arrives with Bunny in tow. The greeting from Bunny is distant, totally devoid of emotion. He's talking about the tattoo he's going to get; he flinches away from me when I reach out to touch his arm in greeting. Judas types in the door code and we walk in without a group smoke. Stood amongst friends I've never felt so alone.

Judas wants to use the first part of my recording session to record some vocals for his recording of the other band I'm involved in with him. RUTT, a band I formed years ago, a cursed band, a thorn in my side at the moment; lost in the shadow of RDI. Maybe that's why they are so offish with me, they fear the monster that I've created for which they play no part except for Judas. Jealously is such an evil creature.

We stand outside a studio as Bunny goes to the toilet. 'Dude,' Judas says. 'I did coke last night for the first time.'

'Right.'

'I don't see the appeal of it, it did nothing for me.'

'Everyone to their own I guess.'

'I generally don't see how people can be so weak as to get sucked into it.'

What the fuck? 'Like I said, everyone to their own. It isn't a question of weakness.' Why do I feel like I'm defending myself from attack?

Thankfully Bunny returns; he and Judas disappear into the live room to set up for his vocals. I can't help but feel put out. This is my studio session to record RDI, not some old project I have no interest in. I put my thoughts to one side and follow the guys into the live room. They're mid-conversation, it falls silent when I walk in. The look I receive tells me I'm currently not welcome. I leave hastily for the sanctuary of the control room.

I sit down in the chair and watch the silent conversation through the glass. I could turn up the channel on the desk to listen but something tells me not to. I just watch casually, mentally counting the cold glances at me through the window.

Eventually they enter the control room. 'We're going for a quick fag,' Judas announces and they leave as soon as I nod my 'okay'. *Thanks for wasting my time,* I add as an afterthought.

What the fuck is their problem? I mean come on, we're here to record, they'd be so pissed if I just fucked around on their time. I push my rough mix CD of the RDI album into the player and sit back. They return just as the bare bones demo of 'Dead in my Eyes' plays. Judas looks at me.

'What's that? I've not heard that one before.'

'You wouldn't have, it's a new track. Like it?'

'Why don't you just concentrate on the tracks you've already got instead of writing new ones.' It isn't a question; it's a statement, a command.

'Because recording an album should be organic. It should grow, and besides, it's up to me what ends up on it.'

'Sounds a bit gay, a bit Dead or Alive to me,' Bunny offers with a laugh.

Judas giggles along with him. 'I can see where that came from.'

'Hey Judas.' Bunny runs up to him. 'Do you take it up the ass?'

'Hell no, I ain't no fucking faggot.' They both turn to look at me.

I just sit there for a moment, lean forward to turn the music off and look back at them. 'Right, on that note, let's get to work shall we?'

I watch Bunny and Judas leave before connecting all the relevant wires into the desk and setting up for recording. Judas returns, I look at him; he doesn't make eye contact as he sits at the desk. Something's different. I sigh. 'You know what to do, I'm going for a fag.'

He looks up, a pissed off look on his face. 'Okay,' he adds nonchalantly. I leave.

Outside I lean against the window sill, often referred to as 'Dom's smoking ledge' given the amount of times I've been seen stood their smoking. I let the smoke rest in my lungs, feeling its euphoria, wishing it was something stronger. I'm at a loss. There is definitely something going on. I can sense it; it's none of this drug induced paranoia. I'm clean and thinking clearly, *seeing* clearly. There's distance, a space, a void around a friendship. I know they're laughing at me. Maybe their tension is like I thought, aimed at RDI, but something inside me knows that Bunny has read my online diary, the warts and all tale of my life outside of our friendship. I know because his change has been so instant and if *that* is merely paranoia then I know exactly how to prove it right or wrong. That plan is sorted. So back to Judas, surely he won't be such a nob over something as trivial as sexuality?

Okay so maybe I'm not worded as 'out' to him but I've never seen it as an issue of being 'out' or 'in', I mean he's heard me talk about guys, he's met all my boyfriends and seen me touch them, he was even there when Ciara came up to me in the pub and was like 'So you and Mark are not together anymore?' IT'S NOT LIKE IT'S BEEN A SECRET. Argh, why can't things just be fucking simple?

I drop the butt of my cigarette and roll another. As I light it I decide not to think.

My daydream lasted longer than I'd expected and when I finally get back into the studio, Bunny has finished as much of his vocals as he can and is getting ready to leave.

'You took your time.'

'Yeah, sorry, got talking to someone,' I lie. They nod; they don't care.

Bunny leaves and I set up for the RDI vocal recording. Judas just paces the control room in silence. The track of the day? The one with a blatant reference to my sexuality in it. How appropriate.

From the live room I watch Judas through the glass as I sing. His head is down; he looks bored. The line is said. 'You bastard son of pain.' He looks up sharply. I can see it, the look, our eyes meet and I know. There's the disgust I've been waiting for. I screw up my lines, the track stops.

'Wanna go from there?'

'No, the beginning.'

I sing; I screw up. I start from the beginning. I want to drum this song's sub-level meaning into his head and I don't care what he thinks. I finish and go and listen back to it. He says nothing. I like what I'm hearing, the direction I've gone in.

'The lyrics are a bit emo,' he states.

'They're honest,' I reply. Who is he to comment on my emotion?

Job done we pack up and leave the studio with a strained goodbye; he doesn't want a pint so I just let him walk away. I roll a joint, sit out of the way on a wall and light up. I'm going to my dad's for the weekend; this is necessary.

The first thing I write on my journal when I get back is: *If you've got a fucking problem with who I am, say it to my face or get the fuck out of my band.*

Who'd have thought it? The message worked. The next time I bump into Bunny, he's there wrapping his arms around me, telling me how the band and our friendship is so important to him. Everything back in place and I don't care what he thinks of my sexuality. The tale isn't so glamorous with Judas. That is even more strained.

I spent a day recording drums for his coursework and before I did so he fluffed himself up and announced that if I'm not careful he 'won't tune up for any of RDI's guitar parts.'

'That's okay,' I reply. 'We've recorded them all.'

'What about the solos?' he says smugly.

'I'll get Mark to record them.' That deflated his ego in an instant, from boner to flaccid in one sentence. Ha.

But the problem is now I'm sat behind the drum kit in a band practice with RUTT that I can't be fucked with and you can sense the tension in the air. Judas' drinking beer and is having a creative low which means every new song he shows us is shit; Ward is just the same, shit; Bunny's doing his best and is the only one speaking to me. This is so fucking dumb. Bunny wants to do some speed with me, Judas' face sums up his thoughts on that. We try to play a new song. It's shit and I say so.

'Well you write some new music then,' Judas spits at me.

'I did and you didn't bother to even look at it, so not my fucking problem is it?'

Ten minutes of silence in a small room filling gradually with smoke from all the cigarettes we're going through isn't my ideal notion of comfort. Judas decides he wants to go home early; we let him. *What's his fucking problem?*

Just as I'm about to go out for fresh air, Ward pulls me to one side. 'What would you do if Judas joined another band?'

'Kick him out of mine,' I reply simply and walk outside. Ward follows.

'Don't you ever think of putting RDI before RUTT.'

I laugh to myself and in his face. 'They're independent of each other and I'll choose whichever one I want.'

'That's not what I said.'

'Well in that case, don't you ever put your other band over RUTT.'

'But I may have to one day.'

'So don't go giving me demands. Whether you like it or not, RDI is my main priority at the moment, and I'm not about to change that.'

'So would you let Judas join another band?'

I sigh. 'Judas can do what the fuck he wants, if he keeps writing shit then I don't want him in this band anyway.'

Conversation over. The other issue highlighted so blatantly. The fear of RDI, the jealousy of it. You know what, I fucking love it, and no I've not been honest to them, RUTT means nothing to me and hasn't for a long time. *Why did I agree to resurrect it?* I hear myself ask.

032

C$_{16}$H$_{13}$ClN$_2$O

The fuckers, that's what they are turning into. Lowdown godforsaken fuckwits. Ok, not all of them, maybe two, maybe just Judas, but I mean come on, give me a fucking break. Here's me trying to get on with recording this album, focusing all my energies into that and I keep getting these pissy fucking phone calls.

The latest has just happened, I'm just lying there and 'ring'. I can't be fucked re-accounting the whole conversation but the basis of it is that cancer in my side RUTT is dropping all its tunes – read as *my tunes* – and the lyrics are to be rewritten so as to remove all swearing. The reason is that Judas feels he is too mature for that now. It's already been discussed with all the other members making me naturally the last to know.

Fuck that, I can't be fucked arguing anymore over it. They want the change they can have it. Kinda feels like I'm being sidelined in my own band. Maybe I'd care more if I didn't have RDI; maybe I'd care more if I hadn't swallowed 10mg of diazepam before the phone call. Maybe I'd care more if I actually cared in the first place. Whatever.

Here's the rope, go hang yourselves with it. Fuck them all.

Okay, a few days pass and I'm all out of diazepam, so un-numbed I got this shit running through my head. Spare me any of this 'I thought you was clean' bullshit; I ain't in the fucking mood.

All I want to do is focus on sitting down and mixing this massive amount of work I've got to finish. It takes up enough of my time, I don't need this pointless shit going on and distracting me because it's the same old shit each and every fucking time. Sort it out then 'puff', same old problems return – read as *Judas' ego*. Want to know how pissed I am? I'm at the point of liquidating. Liquidating forever, to get rid of this deadwood that feels like a ball and chain around my ankle. Not only just the band, but *one* fucking ego in particular.

So, this time he made himself very clear, he's not happy. Well guess what, neither am I. They're not in control, I am. I can end it with a click of my fingers; end it without a second thought.

'Don't feel like I've gone behind your back.' Yeah because if asking their opinions and agreement before getting the courage to phone me wasn't going behind my back then tell me what is.

Get your head out of your fucking ass. You're not in the position to make demands.

FUCK, I REALLY NEED SOME KETAMINE.

dead in my eyes

As you might have guessed by now I'm not really a fan of tension, especially given how I'm generally like 'proper' now, as in I have no chemical boundaries protecting me from the realities of this life. Okay, maybe I should rephrase that to the truth, I don't have a *constant* chemical boundary protecting me. That is why as I'm stood here outside, against my smoking wall, chaining it.

I don't really need to be here, it's not an RDI studio session. My energies could be used better elsewhere but I'm keeping my word that I'd be here as support for Bunny, but I'm feeling bruised so I don't know how I'm going to react to it all. Roll, lick. Click, flame, inhale. Another cigarette burns its way to the grave.

Bunny arrives, he sees a pissed off glare in my eye. 'You alright dude?'

'Kinda.' I pause. Fuck it. 'No, not really. I'm really fucking pissed off.'

'What about?'

'RUTT.'

'Oh.'

'I mean how dare you all tell me what is going to be in my band. Like dropping all my songs in favour of that shit he keeps offering.'

'Dude, I didn't want it to change,' Bunny corrects me. 'Judas called me and said that him and Ward felt the same way and that as the new guy my opinion doesn't count.'

'Of course it fucking counts.' Click, flame, inhale. My hands are shaking. 'I value your opinion above theirs at the moment.'

'Dude I mean it. I love it; I love the direction you want to take it in. He just told me to shut up.'

Bunny's phone rings. It's Judas. Apparently we're late.

'Where the fuck is he?' I ask.

'Already up there.'

So much for the agreed meeting us outside. We finish our cigarettes and move towards the studio.

This is fucking bullshit. He didn't even give us a proper greeting, just rushed Bunny into the live room and is now proceeding to tell me what to do as if I've never been in the studio before. He's even more pissed because I told him it's his project; he can get the sound he wants.

From where I sit I pull out my notebook. I need to get the thoughts out of my head. Lyrics, maybe they'll be a verse, a chorus or whatever but they sound cool. Pen on paper. *I wanna know the truth, and clear all this shit from my mind. I wanna see you burn, lying dead upon the floor. It just feels so numb as to hate you need respect.*

Judas' voice breaks my train of thought. 'I'm going to smoke. I'll leave it to you to start recording. You'll be able to do that right?'

I bite my tongue. 'I'm pretty sure I'll manage.'

He leaves; Bunny and I get to work.

Judas' cigarette lasts about forty-five minutes, when he returns both Bunny and I are sat in the control room.

'Why aren't you recording?' he asks indignantly.

'We did what you wanted,' I reply.

'Really? That quick?'

'Looks that way doesn't it.'

He slams his way to the mixing desk and presses play. His face says it all. He can't complain.

'We're going out for a smoke whilst you check it through,' I state, getting to my feet.

'Really? Well, I'd prefer it if Bunny doesn't smoke.'

'Why's that?'

'It'll ruin his vocal ranges.'

'Err, he was smoking before he got here, what difference would it make?'

'Fine!' Judas shouts. 'Go fucking smoke.'

We do exactly that.

When we return he's sat strumming away on his guitar. I sit down in a chair, Bunny next to me. He pauses and then plays us this new tune. It's shit. He finishes and looks at me.

'That's my new tune.'

'What for?'

'RUTT.'

My heart sinks. He we go. 'Not very RUTT is it?'

'Well, that's the new sound.'

Is it now? 'What? Emo?'

'How can it be emo? It's in drop C.'

'It's still emo.'

'Post-hardcore is more accurate.'

I snort involuntary. 'Yeah, emo.'

'You say emo, I say post-hardcore.'

'I say not in RUTT.'

Judas slams his hand down against all the strings of his guitar violently and looks at me. His eyes say it all. 'Well I don't fucking know what to do then,' he screams, all the toys flying out of his pram.

I sit in the silence that follows without saying a word. I'm not rising to the bait. A moment passes; I turn to Bunny. 'So, where were we? Chorus vocals.'

We get to our feet and leave Judas scowling behind us. Outside the control room we both burst out laughing, trying in vain to compose ourselves before walking into the live room. As we do, I look up. There's a random foam padding hanging from the ceiling. I burst out laughing. 'What retard put that there?'

Bunny looks at me, slightly shaking his head.

'I mean come on it just looks fucking gay and is doing nothing.'

'Judas put it there.'

'Oh.' I turn and look into the control room window. Judas glares at me. I'd forgotten the microphones were on. It really isn't his day.

With him watching I pull the foam down and leave. When I return to the control room I retake my place and pick up my notebook. Judas resumes recording, I let the lyrics fly.

I wanna see you rot, broken, bruised and torn apart. I'm so empty now and you're dead within my eyes.

The studio session continues in almost non-verbal silence. The final icing on Judas' cake comes at the end; not one single CD burner in each of the studios works, they fuck up each disc and he leaves with nothing. Karma.

In truth, in all personal honesty, I have no fucking clue what his problem is. He's just become a right twat, increasingly so. As much as it hurts that it feels like I'm losing my best friend, I really don't have the time to watch him disappear up his own ass. I've seen it before and it's painful.

I've got only one priority now. The same one I've had all year. The Red Devil Incident.

I'm not playing for domination; I can't stand these two-faced lies. I won't give you absolution. We've reached the end of the line.

2006
APRIL

APRIL

034

C$_{17}$H$_{21}$NO$_4$

So here I am, back in Preston. A break from the monotony that is Guildford and all the bullshit that's kinda growing there. Funny that isn't it? All the dust we leave in our wake. Totally independent lives completely unaware of what is being said behind our backs.

Sat once again in my childhood room I think to myself. In the short space of time since I was last here I've changed. My body now marked by the black outlines and shading of my tattoo snaking its way down my entire left arm. My soul marked by all that's happened. I guess the last few months have been a bit of a struggle for me. I've been good, okay a few slip-ups here and there, whether or not they'd be considered major is pretty much irrelevant to me. I dunno; should I really be this open? Do you all have some great opinion of me I could fuck up any more? Again do I care? Should I?

Think, it's all getting pretty lonely, everyone falling away from me with each passing month. Could you say my life's falling apart or that I'm just cleaning? Would a deep sigh clear my mind? Doubt it. I guess I'm a loner. A loner screaming at the world around him.

Okay, I'm a little coked out my mind at this minute, so I guess I still haven't cleaned up like one hundred percent, but at least it's not like I'm speeding along each day. I don't get the speed bugs that I'd feel crawling under my skin, causing me to scratch at imaginary demons. So given where I've been, I'm getting better. Then on the other hand, the lack of being out of it is mirrored by a rise in random meaningless sex, but that's called 'experience' right?

WHY AM I JUSTIFYING EVERYTHING?

I'll shut up now. There isn't any need to justify. To justify is to try and make others understand. I'm just being myself; myself pulling himself back from whatever brink I was in danger of falling off. What I did out of need I now do out of enjoyment. It's all a question of hope.

I'm almost a third of the way through and it's like this awesome secret because, safe of a select few, no one has even heard what I've been working on. It's mine, my baby, and I'm protecting it with all my care.

However I'm at the point I want to be now. The vocals. My time to get all my anger and vitriol out of my system. It's been building and now it's ready to fly, to burst out of me. This is my moment.

It's a lonely journey creating. I turn off my light. It's a pretty much lonely life in general.

crestfallen

I can't do it. Shit, fuck, hell, I can't do it. All the time preparing and I can't commit any of it to tape. It's way too hard. I know what I want but the demons are screaming at me. Digging their claws deep into my back, at my throat, my brain. Total dissatisfaction is a fucking pain.

My mind constantly flicking back to what Adi had said. That he hates my vocals; that I should get someone else to sing it; that I should step away from the helm of the project. You don't know how much that knocked me, really brought me to the brink of tears, but now I'm actually crying. Big stupid tears rolling down from my eyes and I can't stop them.

I've slapped my head so many times that I've got a headache. Shaking so much that I can't even focus. Fuck, why is this so fucking hard? I've listened back to the vocals I've already done and I love them. They fit so fucking perfectly, why can't I do that now? What made them so 'right'? The emotion on them captured so accurately. How? What's missing now? Drugs? Confidence? Why does this self-consciousness have to raise its ugly head right now? The fucking cunt.

Mark's been a fucking awesome help, trying to clear my mind. He was there for me when I first stumbled after Adi's comment. 'Are you going to just give up after one bad comment, or are you going to stand up and stick your middle finger in their face? Isn't that what you do?'

'I can't. I really can't,' had been my reply.

'Oh shut the fuck up,' had been his.

I've kicked him out of the room about god-knows how many times today only to call him back in. Five fucking hours and nothing to show for it. Jesus fucking Christ. I'm fucking angry inside; this should be really pissing easy. Angry Dom screaming and shouting. Nothing. Maybe there's too much unresolved shit going on.

Mark pokes his head round the door. 'How's it going? Any luck yet?'

'Fuck off!' I roar. 'Fuck off. Fuck this fucking shit!' I kick the microphone stand over complete with microphone. 'I'm fucking done. To think I thought I could do this. Who the fuck was I kidding?' I fall onto the floor, head in my hands.

'Earl Grey?' he asks quietly.

I snort a laugh. 'I need something stronger than that.'

Out comes the vodka, the rest of the night written off entirely.

We've decided now to record some clean guitar parts, namely for 'Dead in my Eyes', and Mark being Mark gets them done pretty damn quickly. A simple melody line, forcing a load of retakes just to make sure they're perfect in his mind. Mark, always the perfectionist, which is just the right sort of attitude I want really.

So yeah, what this really means is that now I've got to start thinking about those vocals. Some lyrics can be re-written and I've come up with a few new melody lines, but the question is, will it happen? The simple answer is 'N-fucking-O'.

FUCK.

What is wrong with me? How could I have come this far so confidently and now be in this mindset? Ground Zero of the bomb site that is my confidence. Who ever said words could never hurt you was so fucking wrong. The microphone stand ends up on the floor again.

'FUCK!'

'Just relax,' Mark offers. 'You're trying too hard.'

'Fuck you.'

'Relax.'

Gulp down a whole load of water. Breathe. Calm. Try again. Fuck. Mark gets kicked out of the room.

Alone I sit and cry. Why'd I think I could do this? Was I that fucking stupid to think I could surmount to this level? Am I in danger of being the one who fucks this whole thing up? Should I actually just step back and admit I've bitten off more than I can physically handle? Fuck, this is really annoying. Why am I crying? What good is that to anyone? No one gives a fucking shit. How pathetic I must look, hunched up in this pool of self-pity. This isn't what I do. Okay, maybe it is but not over myself. This isn't me. This isn't the RDI Dom. This isn't me. I'm the carefree brat who doesn't give a shit what people say. I'm the one who'll fight like a pit-bull over something he loves. What must I look like? Walked over? Nobody walks over me without a fight.

I let myself imagine me looking at this scene, kinda out of body. It makes me feel sick. Pitiful. Gollum pining over the loss of the Ring. Whine, whine. Look at me whimper like a scared little boy. Guess what two words are coming? FUCK THAT.

Click, flame, inhale. Breathe in that euphoria; let it burn out all that bullshit. I can do this. I've done it all ready. If people don't like it then tough shit. The Red Devil Incident is my baby and you can think again if you think I'm going to let someone take the helm. My lyrics mean too much to me for them to be sung by a total stranger. It's my emotion therefore it should be bleeding from my soul through my voice.

I call Mark back. He sits, I pick up the microphone. 'Victims of the State' plays through the headphones. My mouth opens; the words flow as intended. 'What the hell have you done to us? Censored what we want to say. Everything you've forced on us, we're gonna throw it back today.'

Kinda the right song to begin with. You know, fighting against those who try to put you down to get their way. This album is not only going to be a fuck you to society, but a big fuck you to those who said I couldn't do it.

Stop commanding life this way; won't stand in line today. Sick and tired of hearing all the fucking lies you have to say.

How about that for a bounce back? I'm kinda blasting my way through the parts like nobody's business. I'm not sure how many I'll end up re-recording but I don't care at this minute, I'm on a roll.

Okay, honest truth is I know most will simply end up as guide tracks but I'm fighting my demons well for a change. Whenever I hear their deceitful little voices I just remember what I'm doing, why I'm doing this. I guess it's a challenge to myself: to prove that I can do this, and not only that, I *will* do it. You're either with me or against me. That's the way life goes.

Confidence is something of a contradiction to me. I'd say I'm confident at what I do, but self-confident? Totally different ball game. The two are not mutually connected are they? Is it merely a case of bravado masking an insecure core? Back to the questions again, shame I can't actually give you the answers.

End of the day, one good thing can be said about it all. I'm still on track. I might be just that tiny bit behind the stupidly big tasks I've given myself – I've decided I want to record a few piano instrumentals, don't make things easy on myself do I? – but it's still all good; it's still all running smoothly. I wish the same could be said about the train wreak that is my life.

2006
MAY

machinations

Second day back into the realm of Guildford and I'm walking through HMV with Mark, my phone rings. It's Judas. Seems weird seeing his name on my phone for some reason. In the past I would have grabbed at it, flipped it open and been all 'Dude! How's it going?' Now I let it ring through to voicemail. I haven't heard from him since the tantrum in the studio, before that he'd been decreasing the amount of time we spent together. The usual Sunday film nights reduced from weekly to zero. The only time he calls he moans. I'm having such a good day; he's not going to ruin it. The phone returns to my pocket.

We're in HMV having just spent the morning in Wetherspoons drinking beer and finally getting round to eating a burger. Which I must say Mark ate a bit too quickly, by the time I'd finished just my burger he'd smashed all his food through his mouth and was sneaking chips off my plate. 'It's coz you talk too much when you eat, it takes you longer to finish,' had been the excuse he'd given, normally that would have worked but today I'd been rather unusually quiet.

Anyway, beers finished, food devoured, nothing of interest in the store we leave. Walking home my phone vibrates in my pocket. A message. From, dramatic drum roll... Judas. I must look confused when I read it. Well, if I did then it was understandable. *Don't forget we've got that audition tomorrow at 5:15.* What the fuck? What audition? Which is exactly what I text back.

Few minutes later a reply. *The one for the festival. Don't be late.* Part of me wants to say I'm not in Guildford, most of me replies with *well it would have been nice to know in the first place.* No reply. Naturally. Once again, always the last to know.

Mark's moaning beside me. 'What?' I ask.

'Dunno, just got a sudden pain in my stomach.' He pauses. 'It's the Fosters.'

'Or maybe it's because you fucking just stuffed your face in like two minutes.'

'No, it was the Fosters. It's poisoned me.'

I can't help but laugh. 'Yeah, that'll be it.' Funny how the news of an audition hasn't got me into a rage. Maybe it's because I genuinely don't care about *that* band. All I want to do right now is go home and try to fit the vocals I recorded into the mixes I've already done. Should prove interesting at least.

At home Mark's lying on the floor as I walk into my room having relieved myself of a piss filled bladder that had been on the point of explosion.

'I've been poisoned,' he mumbles. 'Those fuckers tried to assassinate me.'

'Indigestion?'

'No. Death. Look.' He dramatically wipes his face. 'I'm sweating. The pain is too much.'

'Constipation?'

'No! I'm never drinking Fosters again.'

I giggle and sit at my computer. Ten minutes of mixing pass and he climbs to his feet and rushes from the room. I pause the music. In the bathroom an atom bomb explodes, sending shockwaves across the house. The windows rattle and a cat walking across a fence is blown ten feet into the air. *Constipation relieved*, I think. Then the sounds of bulimia, a finger down the back of the throat job being performed. The bastard's making himself sick.

'Dom!' an enfeebled cry comes across the landing. 'Come here quick.'

'What?' I call back.

'Come here.'

I pull myself to my feet and walk to the bathroom. At the door I speak. 'Bulimic are we now?'

'I didn't force the food out,' I hear him lean to unlock the door. It opens slowly.

'What the fuck?' I'm in hysterics wishing I had my camera. It's a scene of total carnage, sick sprayed across all four walls, and the stench. It's like a corpse has opened its bowels and taken one final stinking shit right on my face. 'What did you do? You are so cleaning this mess up.'

'I did a shit.'

'That I heard and felt.'

'Well that crap came with a fart and the pain left instantly.'

'So, trapped wind?' God it stinks in here.

'But then I breathed in the fumes of Hell and well...' He points around the bathroom. 'I did a bit of redecorating.'

Fuck I really want my camera but it's laying dead somewhere in an unpacked bag. I step away from the door. It begins to close slowly, as it clicks shut I hear Mark say something about cleaning it up. Back in my room I change the track to 'Dirt', I think the title fits the scene.

Day of the audition rolls around and we wake up late. The whole day spent waiting for this thing I didn't even know was happening. To say I wasn't in the best of moods is putting it mildly. I had absolutely no fucking clue what we were gonna play nor had we prepared anything. This was well and truly going to be something.

So, anyway, I drag myself down to the audition being held at Guildford college. I get there early as usual, ten minutes later the rest arrive, they've been sat in the pub for the previous hour and are discussing what we are gonna play. Guess that makes me, once again, the last to know.

Judas' eyes pass over me without so much as a decent greeting. 'You've changed your image again.'

I'm wearing baggy jeans and a black vest top, that's

hardly any different to what I normally wear. 'Hardly,' is what I offer as an answer.

'It's all new though.' With that he turns his back to we to talk to Ward. I look at Bunny and shrug my shoulders. *Whatever*, I think.

So yeah, we get into the room. Judas marching ahead as self proclaimed leader of the band, he's pissed because I changed what songs we are gonna perform. Set up, great, shitty electronic kit which I can't re-wire to be left handed so I'm lumbered with playing open. Judas fiddles with the amp, even though he was told otherwise. Ready. I nod to the band. Count in. One, two, three, four…

What the fuck is that? The band just farts through the first track, everyone losing where they are because all we can hear is Judas' fucking guitar, and what the fuck is he playing? All out of time and baring little resemblance to the tightness we usually display. It's the Judas show and we're just the background.

My eyes connect with Bunny; his face says it all. I look at Judas, his head so far up his ass he can't see anything wrong. I count in the next track. It stumbles and grunts its way flatulently to its end, dying in probably one of our worst performances as a band ever. Buzz-saw guitars with a murmur of something else underneath. If we'd tried to appear professional we didn't manage to achieve it. We look fucking shit.

As we leave the audition room to make our way back in silence, Judas realises he's left something in the room and rushes back with Ward to get it. Bunny and I are left alone.

'Was it me or did Judas just really fuck that up?' I ask.

'I dunno what the fuck he was doing but it was really bad.'

'That's cool, for a moment I thought I was going out of time.'

'No dude, it was him, he put me off as well.'

'What the fuck is wrong with him?'

We shrug at each other then go and wait for them to get back with us. They do, Judas thinks his performance is faultless. Ward and Bunny disappear.

'Dude,' Judas whispers. 'We need to talk to Bunny about his image. I saw him the other day dressed like a punk, that isn't an image I want associated with the band.'

'What he wears outside of a band appearance isn't really an issue.'

'Yes it is. You're just the drummer so yours is not important, but he's the front man, he should always be representing the band.'

'Erm okay, feel free to tell *him* that.'

'Can't you? It's your band.'

'It's not me who has the problem.'

He says nothing just starts fiddling with his guitar. Hello silence, my old friend.

When Ward and Bunny return we all decide it's time to leave. Ward and Judas skip off together in virtual hand-in-hand. Bunny hangs around with a group of kids he knows. I follow a guy who's been eyeing me up the whole afternoon, we find a darkened alcove and he sucks me off. Suck, suck, cum, swallow. At least one good thing happened today.

Just when you think you've got over it, someone always brings him back to you. That one name constantly entering my life. It seems that no matter who I seem to meet I'm always 'that' guy who dated Sam. I'm not really sure I want my past to be known like that. Guess it's nice to know we made such an impact.

Anyway, that isn't the pressing point. I'm sure it'll bumble to the forefront again but at the moment only one guy is pissing me off. Occupying my mind away from the task at hand. Judas. I've ignored a few of his calls but stupidly answered one a few nights back. All he seems to do is moan on about RUTT and all the crap that goes with it and I really don't have the fucking time for it. Ring, ring. 'Hello?' 'We need to talk about RUTT.' Fuck that! So he wants to tell his demands to the band. I'll let him, then I'll do my usual tactic and put them all in the insignificant places.

So yeah, he's on the phone right now. I'm really not listening. Why should I? They can't even afford me that luxury.

'You still okay to meet up tonight?' he asks.

'I said I'm not free Monday nights.'

'For fucksake. Well, Ward works on Tuesdays so I guess we'll have to talk at band practice.'

'Looks that way.'

'Right, I'd better let Ward know then.' The line goes dead. He's just hung up on me.

Well, really, what a fucking jerk. Firstly I don't appreciate being spoken to in an abrasive manner; secondly, it would have been nice to have been asked how I was and have a goodbye. Thirdly, when I say I'm busy on a Monday evening it means I am not free. Why do they expect me to drop everything and go running when they won't do the same? I'm sick of having to fit into other people's schedules, especially when they totally don't give a flying fuck about mine. I am not a dog. I don't come running when you call my name.

Band practice looks like it's gonna be interesting. As you've all no doubt gathered I don't have any motivation for it left, maybe that's because I've been working on RDI for so long or maybe it's because it feels like I'm drumming for a stillborn that should have been aborted long ago. I'm bored of the useless petty conflicts that band causes. However saying that, we can't fuck this band practice up given that we've got that 'festival' gig on Sunday, which again I have no clue about, but as cruel as it may sound I can't help but secretly pray that Judas fucks it all up like he did at the audition. All you'll see is me pissing myself from behind the drum kit.

I'm not amused, like seriously not amused. This is taking the piss, how fucking dare they. Giving us all this 'don't be late, we have important things to discuss' bullshit and then not even bothering to turn up on time. Fuckers. I'm currently sat behind the drum kit, Bunny's on the manky battered sofa. Our faces say it all. We're pissed off with this whole situation.

Ten minutes later Ward walks through the door, a smug look on his big nosed face. A drumstick wipes it off as it connects with his forehead. From the opposite end of the practice room he looks at its source. My hand.

'What was that for?'

'You're late.'

'Judas just called me, he's gonna be late.'

'Look around, I think we've gathered that bit of information.'

'Oh.'

'Yeah, "oh". So we'll just have to start without him won't we?' I look at Bunny. 'Cool with that?'

Bunny nods. Ward plugs in his bass. We start. Judas walks in. Ward puts down his bass and runs to greet him. They hug; Bunny gets a mere head acknowledgement; I just get a look. *Hello to you too, asshole.*

'Can we get on with getting ready for this thing? Given it's only two days away.' My voice cuts across Ward and Judas' heart warming gay greeting. Judas glares at me as he begins to set up. I smirk as he turns his head away. *What a nob.*

The band goes through the motions. Everything played as it should, everything not as it would appear. This is a dead corpse playing a gramophone and it smells like the grave. A big festering pile of shit that hasn't produced any new material because its guitarist is too busy writing material for another band. This is complete and utter ass-wank. The music eventually stops and I drop my sticks to the floor.

Judas and Ward huddle together. 'We're going out for a cigarette,' Ward offers.

I shrug my shoulders; I couldn't give a fuck. They leave without another word. I walk over to Bunny and roll a cigarette.

'What's their problem?' Bunny asks after a drag.

'I think I have an idea of what it is, and what's being said.' I pause. 'But if Judas' problem is me, he has no right taking it out on you.'

'Is he?'

'How many words has he said to you tonight?'

'Erm.' He thinks for a moment. 'Shit, I didn't realise.' The answer is *none*.

'Something stinks. Let's just get this fucking festival done with and then see.'

'This is way too shitty Dom.'

I inhale on my cigarette, hold, breathe out slowly. I raise my eyes to meet Bunny's. 'They're fucking with the wrong person, for one simple reason, I'm beyond caring about either of them.'

end of an era

You know, I really can't be fucked. All this bollocks with RUTT is kinda taking up space in my head that could be used more productively elsewhere. The whole RDI project is coming along nicely, got eight tracks almost complete and I've started work on the videos as well. *That* is where I should be focusing my time, not *here*, waiting for a fucking lift to God knows where.

I was actually hoping that Judas wouldn't call this morning but he did. The plan was I'd of stayed at home and not gone if no one had offered me a lift to the place. I mean I have no fucking clue how to get to the middle of nowhere and nor could I really care, which is something that should be pretty evident to you all by this point. But call he did, so I've had to get ready, grab a few sticks and put my life on hold for the Merrist Wood festival, no let me correct that, what have they called it? Merrist Woodstock. Please, don't make me laugh. A collection of college bands clumped together is hardly worthy of that title.

Anyway, despite my misgivings I've got to be professional about this. A well placed smile and faked enthusiasm goes a long way. Pretend to care just to maintain the simple life. Fuck I'm bored. If there's one thing that would get me running back to my old habits then this is it.

Phone rings. It's Judas. He's here.

What a load of hot air all that surmounted to. Woodstock? What a fucking joke. One drop of rain and panic, main stage closed for health and safety reasons. So instead everyone crams into the safety of a tent – the band's backstage area –

and we're all forced to play in a small corner of it all. Wow, some festival. Band played eventually, being limited to all of three songs to an audience of emo kids and farmers. The performance was actually really good, we played the best we've ever played which was amazing given how shit all the band practices have been up to that point.

Judas confused me today. He was his usual self to me at the start. Like old Judas, none of this bullshit he's been shitting out lately. I could almost say I enjoyed his company again; well that was until Ward showed up and then I might as well not have been there. I don't know, I don't get it. If you're gonna be a cunt then fucking be it all the time and not as a method to show off to some butt-buddy. So now I have no fucking clue what's going on inside their heads. To make it all the more worse, after we performed I might as well not have been there at all. All three of them marched ahead of me like some grotesque threesome and didn't bother to let me be part of their conversation, instead all choosing to make little digs at things I like. The only time Judas said something after was when he fucking had a moan at how much of a pussy I was because I wouldn't hold a gun. The cunt didn't like the reply of 'I'm a man, I use my fists in combat.'

'You'd be no good in the army.'

'I'll never be in the army as I'm not prepared to die for country I hate.'

'Well, if you hate it, why don't you just fuck off?'

'I will at the first opportunity.'

Come on, I mean seriously, why would all this hillbilly farmer shit appeal to me? Why would I want to test drive a tractor, or fire a gun at some round discus flying into the air? So yeah, maybe I was a bit moody, but no difference there right?

I dunno, something is definitely gonna snap soon. You could just feel it when we were all piled in the car at the end. Something just didn't click. Well, if Ward does what he said about getting that band practice next week, we'll have to get everything put out in the open if this shit hole band has any chance of survival. All I want to do is focus on RDI. One hundred percent. Sod all distractions.

Although, if the band hadn't been around I would of let the singer of the first band suck me off like he wanted to.

All it takes is five days for a coward to show itself. That band practice, forget it. That tosser, forget him. That toad, forget that too.

I grab for my phone and call Bunny. He answers. 'Did you know?' I spit down it.

'What?'

'Did you fucking know?'

'Dude, know what?'

'Well, I'm sat here looking at MySpace and it's telling me Judas is the guitarist for Pink Retina.'

'What?' Genuine horror, he didn't know.

'Those fuckers, those absolute bastards. How fucking dare they. How dare *he*.'

'I can't believe it.'

'Check for yourself. So that's what those fuckers had decided at the last practice. They went out and shook hands on the deal. They backstabbed us in our fucking presence.'

'There may be a reason, like he's in both.'

'There is no reason, there is no both. Sorry Bunny but that's the end of it. There is no more RUTT. It's dead and buried and this is the final nail in the coffin.'

'But I love that band Dom.'

'I know Bunny, and that's what's fucked me off more than anything about all this. Judas and Ward screwed you over more because you have nothing to turn to.'

'You sure we can't just get new members?'

'I'm sorry, nope. I haven't got the energy for all that. What's the point in building up just to go nowhere? RUTT is dead.'

'We're still mates though right?'

'Of course we are dude. Nothing changes there.'

I hang up, my mind is still fuming. I guess I could call *him*, but I have nothing to say. What would be the point? Hear more bullshit? Why do people have to change? Why do they always hit a certain part of their lives and turn into egoed twats? Maybe my brain got fucked up along the way, maybe I'm meant to be mature, maybe I'm meant to become nothing more than an ass-kisser who sucks people off to get somewhere. Maybe all those maybes can fuck off to Hell.

The truth of the matter is quite simple. Whatever may have been left of Judas and my friendship has just been pissed out of the system. If there's one thing that I fucking hate it's backstabbing and underhandedness. How dare he go and join Pink Retina, the band he used to say was total shit, and not even have the courage to let Bunny and myself know. Finding out on MySpace, what the fuck is all that about? In all honesty I feel betrayed, total betrayal; it feels like I've just found out someone's been cheating on me. After four years in the band you would think he'd have the decency to say 'Hey, I'm gonna quit.' If not for the band, for the sake of those years of friendship.

I kinda knew this was gonna happen, but to do it behind our backs is just fucking low. I feel sorry for Bunny.

I'm pissed, I've never felt so let down by someone. I mean never. Well, that's it. Our friendship has reached the end of the line. I won't cry for it. He's already dead as far as I am concerned.

The song he wrote for the album. Gone. His guitar parts all now sound like shit. Worthless. Fuck.

here we go again

I'm excited, like really excited. The most excited I've been about anything in ages outside of RDI. The whole Judas-gate has cleared a whole lot of space in my head which has been filled almost instantly with something new. Eeee. Well when I say something, I really mean some*one*. And yes in a 'like' kinda way.

It's been ages since I've been as excited over a guy as this. It's all a bit blind datey kinda. We've been chatting and shit but haven't actually physically met yet. So where should I begin on this one? A name? Yeah, that'll be a good start. His name is Jules, my mate Mark kinda pushed us towards each other. Kinda just clicked. Fuck, I don't know what to do, it's been a while, don't know how to act with all these butterflies. Yeah that's right. I got gay-ass butterflies fluttering chaotically inside of me. Guess that's a good sign right?

So, stood on the Tube with my mate Gemma, oh shit ain't introduced her yet, so remember her just as a name and we'll carry on, I'm too excited for back stories. Right, where was I? The Tube. Yeah, we're heading to Camden for a night out. Jules invited us, well me, but Gem's coming for support.

Stupid excitement sees us skipping down Camden High Street and eventually finding the right place. We queue, I get talking to some drag queen who takes a liking to me and will offer me complements all night whenever she sees me. We slip inside, deposit our bags and find £20 on the floor, how's that for a result?

At the bar I see him, one tilt of the head and there he is. I smile; I know it looks nervous, he returns it. I hear Gem whisper 'he's hot' into my ear. She doesn't need to tell me that.

Drinks bought we bump into him again with Mark. Quick chat and he's whisked away. A joke pout and a look at the dance floor and then the scene stops. Frozen.

We both see each other at the same time. Our eyes connect and our jaws drop. It's *him*. The first time we've seen each other since that Hollywood ending and now we stand here unprotected by the barriers we've put in place. Sam's eyes glaze. He walks away from the scene. The dancing continues. Life continues.

Jules and I share our first kiss in the toilets. I followed him up there, leaving Gem alone to tell any other interested party that I'm a rent boy and charge too highly. So yeah, anyway, the kiss. I just waited for him, grabbed him as he washed his hands and the rest they say is history. We return to the dance floor. Sam so close I could touch. He sees me dancing with Jules and he just stands there. Watching. For a moment I wonder what he's thinking, then my attention is stolen back. He storms off, everyone follows. Jules looks at me, mumbles 'sorry' then follows. I watch them leave, my heart sinks. *Fuck, they know each other.*

I carry on the evening alone with Gem. Shit, I want to cry, scream, punch someone in the face. The minute I go to move on he appears, like a spectre of the past and everything becomes complicated. Everyone's connected, everyone knows each other, one big circle and I wander through as the lonely lover. The one who cannot be forgotten but can certainly be dismissed. Why can't anything be simple.

Gem understands, she tells me to ignore Sam and keep my eyes on Jules. He's why we're here. We wave goodbye at the end of the night. I know we'll meet again. We do, a few days later, we fall for each other in that one day of each other's company and yes, welcome into my life Jules. My new boyfriend. The light in all the shit that's going on at the moment.

Jules, the one person I'll stop taking drugs for just because he asked me to. That level of respect for him and from here on in teetotality from substances begins. No false promises, no slips. Cold turkey stop. Full stop.

2006
JUNE

the end is in sight

I'm back in the studio. Alone, working out how to move on with this album. Recording vocal takes alone is quite hard work, you have to be a quick runner to get from control room to live room, but I succeeded at it. Vocals for two tracks tonight. 'Mutants' and 'Revolution #h8'. The latter being totally reworked to remove Judas' guitars and the former being the new track to replace the one Judas wrote. This is the start of his elimination from my project. The rage is still there burning like fire. Pure anger. Perfect.

Tracks done I go home to continue to work from there. I try in vain to salvage anything worthwhile from his guitar parts and find it an impossible task. A listening of it with Adi for advice confirms it. 'You need to get rid of them,' he says. Fuck. With only eight weeks to go until this album needs to be complete I now have to return to looking at it from scratch.

Don't panic. Don't fucking panic. I panic, without any mind numbing chemicals to mute the severity of the situation I crumble. Ending up sat on the end of a phone line to Mark panicking like a scared little bitch. So much time and effort put into this project and it all unravels at the point of no return, all because I trusted a rotten apple. *Shit*.

'Calm down Dom,' Mark says. 'You'll work something out.'

'Will I? What? This is going to shit. I need a fucking break.'

'Dom, I have the faith in you.'

'You haven't heard any of it.'

'I know, but I know it's awesome.'

I hang up. Scream, huddle up onto the floor and

squeeze out a few tears. *What the fuck am I going to do?*

The phone rings, I answer it. It's Mark. 'I've booked my train tickets. I'll be down when you get back from Download next week.'

'What?' Total shock.

'I'm not letting anyone, even *you*, ruin all this hard work, and I'm not letting you lose your belief in this album. Next week I'm there. We'll sort this out.'

Happiness, complete happiness. A total weight lifted off my shoulders. Once again Bro hasn't failed to show his dedication to the project even though I've kept him and everyone else in the dark with it.

With a smile I delete every single bit of Judas' participation on the album. How's that for a middle finger?

Ohy Dom,

I've been looking at your website and read what you had to say. Time to put things straight. I never 'stabbed' you in the fucking back, if you've got a problem say it to my goddamn face, don't cower behind your website. If anything I've done my best to help you out and scrapping all the guitars that I recorded for you just to spite me, fuck you you're being a petty bitch, and how dare you slate my name and playing on your site when you know that I'm a good goddamn player, certainly better than your lapdog of a brother. Pull your head out of your arse, sort your fucking life out, you ain't a god yet. Ball's in your court!

Judas

Hey dude,

I would of told you at exactly the same point you decided to tell me you'd joined Pink Retina. So yeah, that's wot the backstabbing bit is talking about… it's called common decency.

Dude, before you get on your high horse, I hate to break it to you, but it was actually Adi who told me to re-

record all the guitar parts. It was Adi who said the playing was poor. So you wanna flash your ego at someone go flash it at him coz I don't have the time for it.

As for being God, wow, when did I say that? My head ain't up my ass, when my guitarist hasn't got the guts to tell me to my face that he's joined some band he used to fucking slag off something chronic, then I'm not gonna waste my time with them, it's wot any friend would have done. Criticise my bro, go on, it's funny, think it offends me? At least he knows his place.

So, if anyone needs to get their head out of their ass and take an ego check I'd suggest it be you. You've been on a quest up your own ass for sometime now dude; both Bunny and I saw it first hand, so yeah... I know my priorities, maybe it's about time you sorted out yours.

Dom

20 June 2006

I feel a bit weird today, not stressed, not pressurised, just I feel I want to complete everything at once. I mean I've been working solely on the RDI album now for nine months and now that it is in the final stages I want to spend every waking hour on it – just as I have for the past seven months.

I think I'm just a bit overwhelmed. I feel kinda honoured at the moment. The past few months have allowed me to move forward in leaps and bounds. You know, as my friendship with Judas fell apart I met Gemma, who within the past two months has become like one of the closest friends I've had.

Then Judas picked up his Judas halo and joined some crappy band he has for the past three years constantly referred to as shit, that allowed me to abort the stillborn that was my old band RUTT, allowing me to concentrate solely on RDI.

As all that is happening I meet Jules and well, you know, we go out and next thing I know I feel totally one hundred percent complete.

I'm just so happy with the way everything is, I wouldn't change anything about it, well maybe my nipple rings coz I'm bored of them.

And then you get the symbolic moment of today. In a few hours Mark and I will head down to the studio for what will be this album's last session. That'll be it. Four hours to finalise all parts. That's quite monumental for me. I might cry.

We're done; we finished early. The final vocal takes completed for 'Pain' and 'Life'. The final guitar parts recorded. Rough mixes listened to and they sound fucking awesome. We found out who's in the studio after us. Pink Retina. Judas' new band. That's quite fitting I think. Kinda full circle in a weird way. Judas was in here with me on the first session back in September as my main guitarist, now he'll enter the studio as Mark and I leave. Disconnected from the project yet working in our wake.

All discs burnt, hard drive removed. Everything packed away. Deep sigh and a wave goodbye. This one studio has witnessed so many key moments of my recent past and as I leave it now for the last time I can't help but let a teardrop fall. Clichéd as it is, it remains understandable. Goodbye old friend and thanks for the memories.

7 July 2006

It's done. Completed. Finalised and ready. It almost didn't happen, given that my computer almost died, literally one disc turn from oblivion. If it hadn't been for Jules noticing I would have lost EVERYTHING. Another reason to like him I guess. Big smiley grin at my big shiny new computer.

It's hard to describe how I feel right now with my final CD in my hand. The weirdest part is not having any more mixing to do. Freedom from this computer, but does that mean I now have to re-find the life I pushed aside for this?

Three thousand hours spent on this forty-three minute nine track album. I want to cry. Happy tears. The point I always knew I'd reach, no matter what, has been reached. The line crossed and I've survived. Here to tell the tale. The memories stored and locked away. The rollercoaster of emotions at its end, please make sure you take all your belongings with you when you leave.

Stupid really isn't it? Well, not stupid, just a little bit weird. On this CD is pain, digital recordings of pain and venom spat out as release. Each track containing elements from different moments. Take 'Apathy', the drums were recorded on speed in September, the verse vocals on coke in December, the choruses on nothing in June. Each track has its own story, its own life and all those jigsaw pieces fit together to make this album its complete experience.

Started with amphetamine-fuelled energy, reworked in teetotality and finalised in relationship. So much coke, so much speed, and so much sex hidden from sight by the importance of my drug addiction.

I think Gem summed up this last period perfectly. 'When I started talking to you, you was snorting coke pentagrams. Now you sit at mine drinking green tea and eating walnut cake. How things change.'

Right, time to listen to this CD again.

Twelve days later and the second on-going part of my life is completed. After twenty-one hours of work, my tattoo is finished. How do I feel? Honestly I feel empty, like 'what now?' Everything is finished all at once and this feels like the ending of the 'friendship' I'd built up with the tattooists over the time it took to complete. But at least I have a lasting memento. My left arm a colourful display of, to me, the most beautiful work of art. It sums up this period so perfectly. A roadmap of the journey I've made. Meanings hidden within the art upon my skin. The rune, the skull and flames, the serpent with its autumnal leaves, all merged together, all representing the final stage. I'd burnt myself to nothing and then rose from the ashes reborn and reinvigorated. I made it. I survived.

For the first time in almost a year, I can actually say, hand on heart, I'm happy.

BOOK TWO
JUDAS HALO

august 2006

4 August 2006

'This is amazing. Absolutely fucking amazing.' It's the first time Mark has heard the completed *Self Degraded Suicide* album. Obviously he loves it. 'I can't believe it.'

'Should sound good given the amount of time I spent on it.'

'Yeah I know but wow. I'm really proud of it.'

'There's only one thing though.'

'What?'

'It doesn't capture how I'm feeling right now.'

'How do you mean?'

'It doesn't close this period. I want to write a new EP. All new material.'

'That's easy enough to do. When do you want to do it?'

'Right now.'

'Serious?'

'Oh yes.' And thus begins the work on the new EP.

The music comes naturally and within a few hours the first track is written and ready. All final bits of rage towards Judas spat out and recorded to digital signals. 'Your Judas Halo', new vocal confidence and a new chapter in the Red Devil Incident's history.

Mark records his guitar parts and we sit back and listen. 'Yes.' He nods his head sagely. 'Yes, this is good.'

7 August 2006

Last night a pure yellow moth flies into my room. I befriend it as Mark and I sit and talk. It stays around me all night. Then my dog eats it out of jealousy.

Today, an identical white moth visits us. It sits on my finger before flying away forever. I believe it was the soul of the first one.

17 August 2006

So, the end of another week. Things with Jules seem to have worked themselves out. I mean I was a cunt and he's been moody all week. I've just got some stupid feeling that he's gonna break up with me when I get back to Guildford. I dunno why, I think I'm just scared that he's got bored of me or will cheat. It's just some stupid feeling because he sounds different when he talks to me on the phone, like he can't be arsed or has better things to do. I mean it's probably coz he's tired and shit, but you know, I just have that weird feeling, like he doesn't even sound excited when I'm like 'I'll see you again soon.' It sucks coz I really miss him and it feels like he doesn't miss me at all. I'm just an insecure dick but hey, I guess I'd just like to be someone's first person for once, instead of being second best.

Meh, I wish I could just trust again.

I want to be the centre of your world; I want you to dream of only me, every minute, every second, every day on your mind. But I know I'll never be number one there's always someone more important than I. I wanna be the centre of your world.

20 August 2006

So it seems that almost exactly the same time as last year I find myself single. Yup that's right. Jules and I are no more. And why? Coz he wants to be single and not be burdened by such a moody creature like me, and I'm better off without him apparently.

It was funny; it seemed like such a lame excuse. You know, same words as Sam used last year but I'm not gonna waste my time going after someone who obviously feels nothing for me. So yeah, the thing I've been looking forward to all week and all the time I've been here just isn't gonna happen. Yeah, he's gonna come pick me up but that's it. Isn't gonna stay or anything. I feel empty. Hollow inside. What's the fucking point you know? I think I find the one I want and now 'pfft', nothing, alone. Looks like the five-year cycle is on track.

Yet another person takes my heart and just simply throws it away. Use me, get bored and then throw me away. Have your singledom, you'll be happier without me.

Why should I expect anything different? I'm crap, I'm never gonna have someone feel for me what I felt for them. I should just accept that. No one gives a fuck about Dom.

I think that's what hurts the most. The fact that someone can say how much they like you, want to be with you, and then they just dismiss all that as 'meh, it was nothing.'

So stop and listen to my heart, it's crying out for some control. Someone to love, someone to hold. Someone who feels what I feel. Pray, please pray for me. Pray, I pray for you. Pray into the silence. Pray.

25 August 2006

Why is it that the things I always look forward to always get pulled away from me? It's like God's joke, dangle the carrot of happiness in front of my face but never let me get to it.

I was happy, and now there's nothing but this, an empty hole inside me. Sat alone. All those words cast aside as meaningless. How could you truly feel that for someone and then wake up one day and go against it all?

So I look forward to seeing Gemma, but that's out the window. I have to wait, our date replaced by a guitar lesson that obviously is going to take up all her afternoon and evening, leaving no time for a chat with me. So I have to wait until Friday when it's best for her to meet me. Dom fitting his life once again into the timetables of others. No one puts Dom first, even a guitar is more important than me.

The future I want to achieve lies in the hands of people I've never met. People who don't know me. People who don't even exist to me are in control of my destiny. Them feeling like gods with people's hopes and dreams made or shattered by their decisions.

Dom's life, a life that is governed by the decisions of others. A life where all the dreams are reliant upon what other people feel is appropriate. You sit and think how happy you would be if everything worked out the way you wanted. That people cared about you as much as you them. You sit and think about it all and want to cry.

Even your own life isn't in your control.

28 August 2006

I refused Jules a hug and now I'm crying. I turned down the last chance to hold him. Why? Why the fuck did I do that?

One phone call and everything is sorted. Peace of mind snorted up the nose in grainy lines.

So here's my heart, there's your foot. Stamp it down, shatter the burden of me and be freed from the shackles. Move on. I look down at the shattered remains, don't know if I can be bothered putting it all back together, that way it can't be broken again.

I pick up a shard; send it in a letter to the cosmos. Maybe they'll send Mothra to bring peace and harmony to my soul. Happiness in this life? Maybe not. Still got to work my way through the karmic retributions of a past life. Happiness in the world of Dom? Don't be stupid little Pisces boy.

Twenty-three years in and tired. Bored. The prospect of another twenty-three of this shit sends shudders down the spine. To deal with a never-ending cycle of getting close to people just to have it thrown back in the face. Get bored of me; move on, leave alone and meh. Not like I blame them. I feel the same way about myself. I wouldn't even inflict my burden upon people. Maybe this year I'll open the door to the darkness, let it engulf what it couldn't six years ago.

Stupid Pisces boy swimming in your toxic pool, your brain in the clouds. Listening to other people's problems, dealing with their shit. Would they do the same? Don't be stupid. You Pisces come last. Never gonna be anyone's number one. Not even your own.

Stop the train, I wanna get off.

Hello room, hello Guildford. Hello life. This world's ending one minute at a time.

september 2006

03 September 2006

Oh, this is weird. I mean I was gonna write about this date I had on Thursday which went okay but nothing special, but instead now I've got to write about Sam.

Yeh, I met up with Sam yesterday. We had a chat, caught up then went to Rebel Rebel and I stayed at his. It just felt as though we hadn't split. Like it was just a week since we last met.

So yeah, I guess that's the complication of the year. When we fucked he told me he loved me. I told him the same. It just feels right when we're together. It hurts you know, we're so good and it's obvious we won't get back together. I guess I have to be satisfied that I've found someone who I love but can't have, or rather had and lost.

It was so funny to see people's faces when we were together. It was kinda like 'What the fuck?' Jules challenged Sam with a 'So you're here with Dom are you?' I didn't even talk to him. I had such a good night. We still bounced off each other like usual.

I think what made it worse was that we both said we felt the same, and, you know, shit happened. My dick spat up his ass twice. But at least we got shit sorted out. Whether or not I see him again is a different matter. Maybe it's better to let the past stay in the past. We shall see how it all pans out. I'll most likely never hear from him again.

Dommy Lee and Samela Anderson. Forever in love, separated by fate.

04 September 2006

Wake up. Move. Get out of bed. Shower. Clean. Look at my arm and inspect the mark which I noticed above a vein on my right arm yesterday. Maybe it's nothing. If only I could physically care enough.

Pick up iPod, stick on shuffle and leave. Bag slung over my shoulder. Guildford busy even though it's only turned 10. Buy what I need and sit by the castle. Smoke. Breathe in, out. The grass is damp.

Home. Missed call from a private number. Drink tea, listen to more music. A soundtrack for the day.

05 September 2006

I'm dreaming, screaming when everyone else has woken up. A faded halo hanging crooked above me, a message no one wants to hear, a life's meaning hidden within the tattoos on my arm.

I sit here, thinking. If you look into the shadows long enough you can see it reflected back at you. Something lurking deep in the depths of the eyes. Pain, understanding, knowledge. A film camera recording onto the soul.

I sit. Waiting, willing. If no one thinks about your existence, do you actually exist? A faded memory to match the faded halo. A crown of thorns pushing down, drawing blood. We all have a cross that we must carry. The weight of life pushing you down into the dirt.

Life on a cycle. Tired. Bored. Wishful. Head in the clouds, never tied down. Each day a step closer to the end.

People chosen. Key pieces in a divine game. Pick up my piece and play it. See how brightly I will burn. Shatter the halo and then watch me crash to the ground once my task is done.

Please do not stick pins in the walls or furniture.

07 September 2006

The scent of filth in the air. A door open, the smell of madness and despair. Poverty shown through phone calls and fevered shouts of rage. Remember the knife. Remember the video. Remember the wallowing pity oozing from the pit.

Push my door closed. Cut off that world. Pick up the brush. Sit and think. Colours on a page. A vision from the mind. A photo of the soul. Pigmented emotions leaving their mark. Permanent, even when covered over.

Cigarette burns low. Breathe in; breathe out. Air filtered through death. Mouth dry. Need water. Maybe later. Let it form a desert and then go in search of the metal oasis. Life on a tap.

Stop. Look. Listen. Remember the green cross code.

11 September 2006

This day 2001. Satisfaction. A new life started. Moved to Guildford. World events little more than a footnote. A passing comment in a diary once written never re-read. Five Septembers on. Still here. Five years to build a reputation.

This day 2006. Satisfaction. Look back over a year. Memories burnt digitally onto disc. Music from the soul. A body recovering from abuse. A year. A year locked away with myself. I exploited, burnt out and then rose from the ashes only to be sat here using again. Confident. Arrogant. Calmer, maybe. The darkness touched me and left a stain. This is my honour.

Reputation is what other people know about you. Honour is what you know about yourself.

Get up. Switch on computer. Check emails. Message from Mum. Makes me smile.

'Well done. It is five years today since you moved to Guildford to follow your dreams. Don't lose sight of it. You will get there in the end, but hell I do miss you.'

172

003

Difficult to predict.
One moment I'm in my own happy universe,
The next I'm on a bad trip to my own personal hell.
So peace of mind can't be bought.
It's merely a question of control.
Don't bite the lip too hard
Or scratch the skin too deep.
For what flows out
Something must go back in.

september | october 2006

17 September 2006

Acid drops falling from the sky, corroding everything mankind has created. Demons praying on the souls of the already dead. Life in tedium. Faded dreams, jaded, wasted. Show me your god and I'll tell you what he did to me.

I walk in limbo, disconnected from everywhere, from everything. Watching, observing. Everywhere strict guidelines, mechanical people moving at mechanical pace. Creatures on their shoulders, controlling, dictating. Morals beamed like text messages into their minds. Brains connected to the master server, slaves on painkillers. The love of one dismissed for the lust of many.

All around me are faces. Each face containing seven, one for every deadly sin. Their mouths stitched, their eyes empty sockets; sowing needles through their ears. The wise monkeys of the modern age. Saying nothing, hearing nothing, seeing nothing. Skullfucked and empty. Pawns. Usable, disposable.

Sit on the floor, the centre of a roundabout. What of me? Where do I fit in? Has my purpose been served and now all I can do is observe or join? Is my card still to be played and this is the wait? Gather information, learn. My halo a crown of thorns on my head. So I wait and listen to others, expecting nothing in return and getting just that. No one wants to see the world through my eyes, but if I had the choice, would I?

Mother please explain to me why this would has become so twisted and bitter. Lives twisted between time and money. Dreams forgotten for material gain. Voices inside my head, feeding me fear, feeding me doubt. Losing my faith. So

I'm out of control? Each tick of a clock a second closer to the end.

Still on that roundabout waiting. Waiting all the time. A whole lifetime of waiting. Nothing is instant, join the queue and be patient. Good things come to those who wait. Really? Maybe I have to wait some more.

Waiting for everything. Waiting for everyone. Do they wait for me? Don't be stupid. I'm put on hold. Sit in silence. Wait. Disposable.

Well fuck you all.

18 September 2006

To be a child again. To live a life without care. Would I do anything different? Would I grow up as someone else? A life without real pressures yet a series of events that can change your whole future.

Our past is what makes us who we are. Even the slightest alteration would bring about massive change. Place us in new situations. Would those be better? You'll never know.

Even this current state I'm in, a catatonic wait for something to happen, will be having an effect of my future at some point, even if my future looks like a perpetual wait.

The next phase of life is around the next corner, but it depends on how long the road leading up to it is. But no matter it's getting closer, one day it will be there, waiting to be walked down.

Flick onto autopilot and enjoy the ride.

19 September 2006

Reach a certain age and act that way. Noticing that in others. Maturing just because it's expected. Mature to fit in. Is it wrong to be immature and hyperactive? Age is meaningless to my attitude. I feel the same as I did when I was fifteen. More life experiences but the attitude remains. Feel dragged down by people's maturity. Fun replaced for sophistication.

It's horrible to see it. Sit and watch. Brain saying 'fuck

you're acting old.' Mouth shut, just go along. A few sly lines and pray it doesn't happen to you. Be true to yourself and you will find inner happiness. To conform is to die. You will murder who you are to be what people want you to be.

Accept me for who I am or don't accept me at all. I change for no one. I've taken that route before and never again will I do so. I promised myself that.

So how do I feel at this moment? Honest truth, I feel nothing. Empty. A life without purpose. Just existing, existing on the mind of no one. Sitting, well actually lying here forgotten. A toy in the attic. A distant memory.

People move on, no one takes me with them, so why do I feel the need to take people with me? The curse of mankind, dispose of a person once their use has been achieved. The curse of Dom-kind, to be the one who is always disposed of. A never-ending circle of being used.

Thanks for the fun, see you later. My burden obviously too heavy. Now I don't chase, I don't try to cling on to those who dispose of me. If they don't want me to be part of their life then fine, see you later. I'm either there or I'm not. You can't have it both ways. I'm not the person you turn to when no one else can be bothered with you.

I'm not a dumping ground for all your shit. If you're not going to care about my problems then I'm not gonna give a shit caring about yours. What would I have to gain for doing that?

So there's a hole in my soul. I don't feel complete and I know that's not gonna be something I'll ever feel again. Exist without a centre. But at the end of the day that's my problem, I mean no one else cares do they? Everyone is so consumed with themselves. Self-centred assholes.

From now on, it's my way or the highway. Well that is until I get suckered into being used again.

Today I asked the sky a question.

It said: 'Beware the moon, it steals light from another.

Allow the sun to guide, but if you look too close you'll get torn asunder. Its brightness will illuminate the way but you must take a path of your own choosing. Just follow the stars with caution, for they are only reflections of the truth, shadows which could be lying.'

22 September 2006

Look buster, okay we fucked but here's how it works. I'm cold, cold hearted and dismissive. You had your use now get lost. Sex. Sex out of relationship is meaningless. Don't ask me questions about relationships, don't ask me to start hanging out with you, I don't even want to know your name. If we've fucked then you're not my friend. I respect my friends.

You're not special, just glorified masturbation. You're just a piece of meat to me, on the same level as a blow-up doll. I was most likely thinking of someone else when we were fucking.

There remains no vacancies for relationship, and even if there was don't think you'll get anything from me. I hang my love around my neck, you've gotta be something truly special to get that close. Good luck in trying, everyone has failed so far.

Giggle, laugh. Serious face.

03 October 2006

These feelings won't fade. As strong today as they have ever been. And it hurts. This hurt won't fade; a vacant emptiness at my core numbed my chemicals. This hurt grows stronger everyday.

I want to be the centre of your world.

06 October 2006

So is this reincarnation? Paying for the sins of your past. Life an eternal torment. Your desires, hopes and dreams dangled like carrots in front of you. Handcuffed arms behind my back, forced to look, watch everything happen with no ability to reach out and touch. Faces smiling, laughing at my struggles. Back to that padded cell, doctors watching as I walk, pace around that confined room, my eyes seeing my world. Madness catalogued and filed. Electrodes attached to my head. Shocks designed to bring me back to reality.

Step by step. Pacing, rocking, unstoppable. No escape. How can you trust people when you can't even trust yourself? They take, they screw, they rob. Still moving forward. Time passes by. Even your own body decays around you. You exist for all but a few moments and then you're forgotten by the world that created you.

I'll wait here. Stand here on the wall. Hanging by a thread, supported by a spider's web. Create the soundtrack in my mind and listen to everything that's said, but I'll absorb nothing. A stray in the gutter, a burden on your soul. From this wall I feel closer to Heaven. Mother please tell me I can be an angel so I can cut off my wings in protest and fall from the heavens. Shatter the halo and cross through into a garden of snow. Ebony snow stained by my bitter blood. Red on black. A devil's head will rise and I shall be born again.

10 October 2006

Silence. Silence speaks more than words. So I thank you, in your silence I have learnt more than a thousand pieces of wasted air could say.

You hold my heart in your hand but you'll never set it free.

15 October 2006

A needle falls from the sky. Spinning, turning through smog filled air. It lands point first, tearing through skin. One needle mark hidden upon an arm scarred by millions. So this is euphoria; this is calm; this is clarity. Creative bliss, it's all pouring back to me.

An epiphany.

A pink elephant in the room.

Nightmares. I've had nightmares every night for the past two weeks. Nightmares within nightmares. Have to wake up three times before you finally hit reality. A fear to go to sleep. Once awake, shadows, figures creeping at the corners of your eyes. Waiting for the snap of fingers to wake you from a coma. The barriers are blurring.

Through the needle prick I pull the crack wider. If you exist on the Otherside, you don't come back cleaner.

BOOK THREE
JUDAS INFERNO

march 2008

The world shatters, everything crumbling around me. If one pill can make you larger, another small, then the pile in front of me could bring about salvation and end it all. So lost, alone. No direction. No escape except through the exit. The last time I felt this low was over eight years ago, sat here in the same room. Is anyone listening? 'No.'

Back then I'd picked myself up, this time, well I dunno. The past six months have been marred with rejection after rejection; hatred and disgust; the death of a surrogate mother. These walls have been falling for sometime but now they've crumbled to the dirt. This could be an ending or a new beginning. Who knows?

I remember speaking to Jackie about her cancer; she'd said the sweetest thing. She said 'I want to go before Len because I know he can cope without me. I know that I'd be lost without him.' You could hear the love in her voice; you could tell she meant it with all her heart. When you saw them together you knew that they were the centre of each other's world.

You see that and then you wonder about your own life. Lost and abandoned with your memories. Will you have someone who loves you by your side when you're old and frail? Someone who you've loved above all else, shared so any constant good memories with, who stuck by you through all the bad times like you did them. Or will you die alone, empty hopes filled with tears of the past, no one to remember you once you're gone.

Fuck, this house feels so quiet.

Search for a reason, a feeling, anything that could

justify an emotion. You search but cannot find. No connection, nothing. Maybe it's because I've become so cold, so distant, filled myself with so much disgust towards mankind that I cannot see past the superficial trappings of first opinions. I used to be so caring, easy to fall for someone. Now I'm jaded, damaged, a heart too scared to break. Maybe my heart still belongs to another; if not the person then the memories. So much for people to live up to. Memories are a hard nut to crack.

Tell me please why I should still care about the other? Tell me why this fucking heart hasn't healed, why the hollow core still rattles with the memory of a face. The ring has left the finger but the promise remains and the flesh is tattooed. Tell me why it still hurts. Tell me why I should still care about them when they stopped caring about me long ago. Tell me why, please fucking tell me why.

And this life remains on hold. Progressing nowhere, little steps here and there. Just one life swirling to oblivion.

So many questions and no answers. I've lost sight of happiness and fill it with trivial things to keep my mind off how fucking alone I am in the world.

Always searching to find the truth behind this life. Wishing for nothing, but dreaming for something. Answer that you God of Lies, is there a reason? Is their a meaning to standing around in all this shit? And if I stumble what then when there's no one around?

Watching someone dies before your eyes is horrible, each day preparing for the worst. Everyone leaves in the end. Silence, so much silence. Hello silence my old friend, I'm cooking a mini roast for dinner, would you care to join me?

Stupid boy and your solitary memories of one boy and his iPod, such a lonely existence. So much silence.

Jackie died and I never got to say goodbye.

We fill our lives with so much noise, so much sound. Build a soundtrack to our lives but it's all self made. In those pregnant pauses, those moments when everything stops you realise there is only silence. Without noise your head is cleared, thoughts crisp. The pain magnified. In those moments you realise how small you are, how alone, glimpses of eternity silently waiting in the distance.

The morning after she died I awoke at sunrise. New light rising silently above the houses opposite, growing, bringing the hopes of a new day. In that moment I realised everything keeps on moving. Life continues until that moment the silence comes to surround you. So you pick yourself up, store those memories and grieve alone for the loss of someone dear to you.

If I sit here now and think of my situation I'm lost. I cry myself to sleep; I have no interest in anyone or anything. Not even my boyfriend. He's just there, part of this rubble and I can't work out where to place him. I wonder, if I'd done things differently in the past would it have made all this better? It would be better to be anyone else but me. Lonely old me. Forgettable me. So, if you're listening should I keep falling? Keep trying? Should I continue living hating myself with every breath?

Come on, somebody help me. Save me. I don't want to be alone.

Mark wrote a new tune at my request. Music now the only way I can release my emotions. I cried when he walked into the room, I cried even more when he showed me the tune. Oh my god, it was perfect. The lyrics poured out and it was recorded in one take. All the emotions pouring out and spat through the microphone. My tears streaming down my face. I broke down and cried, stood there and all that upset just melted out of me. Despair, everything. Music, my salvation.

The quickest turnaround of a song. Mark returns in the morning, he's taken time off work to make sure that I'm not going to be alone in this state. I play him the track and he is speechless. I cry, breakdown again and he pushes all the dirt away to give me a hug. I cry in his arms. Once again I've burnt myself out, once again Mark is here to help. I couldn't ask for more, in this moment this is all I need.

The track is played again. This time I don't cry; just sit smoking a cigarette in quivering hands. Inhale; exhale. Already I feel lighter.

So I'll ask you again heavens. Eight years since I last called up to you, I hope you're listening now, could you understand if you are? Do you like seeing me here alone? Crying, praying, screaming into the dark. I'm rotting, self-destructing once again but at least I'm clean. I have been for a while now.

My direction has been lost. The only constant is my boyfriend. Do I love him? I think so. Can I see myself without him? Yes; that's honesty. As much as he loves me, I don't know, there's a connection missing. Something that causes me to just snap and scream at him. Maybe it's the lingering ghost of the past which by being with him is constantly crossing my path. I know I should try to make things work, maybe once my head is cleared it will. I'll re-find that element that made me want him in the first place. Who knows? But you shouldn't give up on a person right?

Stupid isn't it? There's certain things that define your life, certain elements that remain a constant. For me that seems to be one thing, one person who constantly plays a part in my existence no matter what. A ghost in the corner, a part of my soul forever, but what a beautiful constant, to have met the one person you truly loved and to always have their presence with you in memory or person. Love born from a soul meeting, two halves once joined in perfect harmony. Maybe it isn't the person, they just personify the 'thing', the real constant at the core of this, all of this. Love. True love. The warmth of that love. I used to believe you can only love once, maybe that is true, maybe not. For all I know an even stronger love may be just around the corner waiting to break this old bond with something new. Something better. They always say that the point at which you break is the point the tide will turn. Unfortunately for my boyfriend I know he ain't the one. The past is hidden in the shadows; the future waits in them.

So, what is there for me now I've lost my way? There's no dreams in my head and without dreams there is no future. I used to fear the day I would sleep and see only black, well, that day has arrived. So should I embrace the shadows? Pray salvation; swallow all these pills and wait, hoping everyone will forgive me once my candle fades? I'm dead. I feel dead. Tired and fed up of everything. Who actually gives a fuck about me and my stupid fake smiles? I'm bored of wearing a mask.

All I want is freedom, peace of mind. Maybe an answer, but definitely a reason to be here. All I see is sickness, a constant screaming. I want to be someone else. This world is killing me.

I'm nothing but worthless dirt.

BOOK FOUR
WORDS

apathy

Sold our souls to watered deception,
Allowed no truth with moral inflections.
We didn't agreed to this domination,
But we're gonna follow anyway.
Told no truths but dressed it like candy,
Televised hatred, your pollution was easy.
We didn't want it to be like this,
But we took your bribery anyway.

Dictatorship, need permission to protest,
A vote for you took away our freedoms.
You didn't tell it would be like this,
But we eat your poison without say.
Herded up like lambs to slaughter,
Turn on TV, let celebrity blind us.
We didn't agree to this extermination,
But you cut our throats anyway.

I don't want it to be this way,
I don't want to die today,
I don't care if you take me away
I'm just here to have my say.
I don't want I to be this way,
I don't want to die today,
I won't kill in your name,
Fight your wars with your own pain.

Terrorised, that is what you tell us.
Petrified, that is how you want us.
Sympathise, this is how you blind us.
Apathy, is this how we wanna be?

dead in my eyes

I wanna know the truth,
And clear all this shit in my head.
I wanna see you burn,
Laying dead upon the floor.
I'm gonna take my time
To word all the thoughts in my mind.
It just feels so numb,
As to hate you need respect.

I'm not playing for domination,
I can't stand these two-faced lies.
I won't give you absolution,
We've reached the end of the line.

So wipe the tears from your eyes,
There's nothing more to say.
I pull the knife from my back,
You're dead in my eyes.

I wanna see you rot, broken,
Bruised and torn apart.
I'm so empty now
And you're dead within my eyes.

revolution #h8

We are the ones you hated, the faces you mutated,
We take your morals and throw them away.
We are the self-degraded, the ones you want aborted,
We know that you wanna abuse us today.
We have that hidden beauty; our faces are so dirty,
We got a freedom you can never have.
But we're so fucking wasted, we are so fucking angry,
We take your bullshit every fucking day.

You are the ones who made us; you spread your legs and
        pushed us,
We are the product of our mother's cunts.
We are the ones who made it, the ones who entertain you,
We're fucking up to your applause.
We know that you can't stand us, we know you fucking use us,
Well know that we fucking hate you too.
We know you wanna beat us, but know that you can't touch us,
Watch as we undress ourselves this way.

You are the ones who fear us; we are the souls of deceit,
You are the figures of morality.
Political correctness surrounded by defeatists,
Come try stop us today.
This is our fucking war song, we are a fucking army,
Marching on in unity.
Our freedom is our virtue, we campaign against you,
Gonna smash your society.

This is our revolution.

The time has come to spread our wings.
This is our evolution.
We don't care about what could have been.

sell your religion to the mutants

Heard all this shit before,
Been promised our salvation.
All your promises, all your twisted truths,
Get lost in our confusion.
We heard your god hates us
For our sinful solutions.
All we've ever been, all we've ever seen,
Cleansed with your absolution.

Heard all this shit before,
Been shown our salvation.
Just a wasted life, just a place in hell.
Dropping bombs to kill a nation.
We heard your call for us
But we don't need your quick solutions.
Never wanna be, never gonna be
A slave to your pollution.

Sell your religion to the mutants
Coz all we know is this pain and suffering.
Sell your religion to the mutants
For all we see are your lies and dysfunction.

The time has come,
Choose your side on the new battleground.
Raise your fist, sing in time,
March on our battleground.

We know what we want,

We know what we need,
We know everything we need to know.
We know who we are,
We know what to say,
We know everything we want from you.

dirt

There's a question I ask myself, am I still a man?
Degraded thoughts of suicide killing who I am.
Betrayed by the future, abandoned by my past.
I just need some time.

The question on the lips of man, why am I here?
Will I be remembered for being who I am?
Hated by too many, forgotten by my friends.
Please give me a chance.

I'm nothing, nothing, nothing.
I'm nothing, nothing, nothing.
I'm nothing, nothing, nothing
But worthless dirt.

how do you feel now?

How do you feel right now?
A river flowing regret?
You bastard son of pain,
A blackened whore within.
And why couldn't I see?
Like mother, like child.
The poisoned web of lies,
Deceit runs in your veins.
It resides in your mind,
A tumour set in your brain.
To be used once again,
To start living that lie.
So how do you feel now?

Did you bother to think?
To take a thought of me?
When you woke one day,
Alone and set free.
I was bleeding inside,
The razor cut through the skin.
I tried to rip out my heart
And then awoke from that dream.
So how do you feel now?

When I think of you now,
I see a lost lonely child.
I hope that you're sky high,
I hope you got what you want.
I'm glad you set me free.

So how do you feel now?

life

Rosie girl contemplates suicide,
This is how she goes with so many pills inside.
If you could see the pain in her eyes
Then you would know that there's nothing left inside.

Tommy boy wonders where is the fun,
That letter wrote then he picks up daddy's gun.
If you could see the pain in his eyes
Then you would know that there's nothing left inside.

Tears in eyes their sickness never dies,
Tormented souls, life crying out in pain.
Oh please God don't say that their lives were in vain.

009

13-11-00

I hope you're listening now,
A little late but I can't complain.
I want to ask you why
You left me to rot away.
Back then I was so scared,
My prayers not good enough it seems.

You turned your back that day,
Gabriel just closed his eyes.
Your son Christ turned up the TV,
So no one saw what was happening to me.
I was crying for you, screaming out for you,
Hoping for a miracle, praying one would arrive.

I just want you to know,
I'm left scarred,
Demons still in my head.
Maybe I'm just so bad,
The weed strangling the corn.

sick and tired

I'm sick and tired of living this lie,
I'm sick and tired of wanting to cry.
Nobody cares as I rot away,
Forced not to have any say.
Darkness surrounds me
But what will I see
When everything fades to black?

I can't breathe,
I can't see,
I won't be anything but me.

All of this anger,
Why won't it fade?
Is this why I have been made?

I'm sick and tired of living this lie,
I'm sick and tired of wanting to die.
Nobody caries of I go this way.
Needle in arm, knife on a vein.
Darkness surrounds me
But what will I see
When everything fades to black?

in dreams we sleep

I see the darkness surrounding me,
Feel it wash the pain away.
Want to see the truth someday
But got lost along the way.

Been told far too many lies,
Taken the beatings in my head.
Want to know what I can be,
But I'm far too easily led.

In my dreams it seems so real, I touch the face of God.
In my dreams it seems so clear, but I know

Eternity weeps, as the Son of Man sleeps,
And it cries out for me.
Eternity weeps, as the Son of Man sleeps,
And it's crying out for me.

pain

I feel so empty inside,
So used and discarded.
Everything I felt seems so meaningless
But that's how it had to be.

I saw the photo and cried,
Felt something rot and die inside.
He stole a kiss that should have been for me
But that's how it had to be.

Cry with me; lie with me,
Tell me how it's gonna be.
Cry with me; lie to me,
Tell me how it's gonna be.

Need something to heal these scars,
Need something to make me numb,
I don't want to live in this pain anymore.

your judas halo

They say, you do.
Payment doubled for your regret.
So you did and they smiled,
Happiness in your deceit.
You turned; it died.
Pushed the knife in the back.
It burnt; it smashed
The stupid promises carved in stone.

And I can see you now, sat upon your throne.
You swapped a crown for a Judas halo.
And when you're rotting there,
Rope around your neck,
I hope you see your Judas halo.

You sit, a king,
A whore I will never mourn.
You fell.
Ego.
A broken shadow is what you've become.

And I can see you now, sat upon your throne.
You swapped a crown for a Judas halo.
And when you're rotting there,
Rope around your neck,
I hope you see your Judas halo.

centre of your world

So I wanna word what I feel inside,
Lay myself bare upon a stage.
Do you wanna hear?
Do you wanna know?
Or is it just too much for you to take?
It's hurting me,
I can never have all the devotion I give to you.
Are you listening?
Do you really care?
Or are you just out busy with your friends?

So here's my heart, would you take?
Or would you just throw it away?
Would you stand by me?
Stand before the rest?
Or would you follow them so blindly?
Can you spend a day
Without a thought of me?
Remembering only by a message I send.
So I'm missing you,
You say you feel the same,
But why does it feel like you're bored of me?

I wanna be the centre of your world,
I want you to dream of only me.
I wanna be missed, at least be loved,
Every minute, every hour, every day on your mind.
But I know I'll never be number one,
There's always someone more important than I.

I wanna be the centre of your world.

promise

Do I run away to escape from this pain?
Gotta find a way to heal this heart.
It feels so cold today, the death of my soul.
Lost eternally, but I don't know
What to do, what do I say?
What to feel when this world ends,
It ends today.
Don't know what to do, don't know what to say.
What to feel when my world dies,
It dies alone today.

Standing lost I pray to the God in the sky,
Is he listening or has he turned away?
So alone today, where are all my friends?
Lost eternally, but I don't know
What to do, what do I say?
What to feel when this world ends,
It ends today.
Don't know what to do, don't know what to say.
What to feel when my world dies,
It dies alone today.

What about me? Did I matter?
These emotions are wasted.
When you promised, did you mean it?
Or was it a lie?
Feeling lost now, nothing changes.
Lying dead in my arms now.
And my heart beats, though it's shattered

On these broken promises.

pray

Standing tall I look upon
A wasted love that lingers on.
Dismissed away as though I'm nothing.
A final wish that never comes.

Stop and listen to my soul,
It's crying out for some control.
Someone to share, someone to hold,
Someone who feels what I feel.

Pray, please pray for me.
Pray, I pray for you.
Pray into the silence.
Pray.

save me

I wish for nothing, keep dreaming for something,
I'm praying to the God of Lies.
Always and ever, searching to find it,
The truth behind his life.
Is there a meaning or is there reason
To standing around in all this shit.
Somebody save me, somebody help me,
I'm losing in this deadly game.

I cannot take this, no I cannot face this,
Waking each day with regrets.
If I'd done it different, would it make it better,
Been anyone else but me.
Do I keep falling, or do I keep trying,
Hating myself with every breath.
Somebody save me, somebody help me.
I just don't want to be alone.

Save me.
Save me from myself.

lost

Is anyone listening?
Could you understand?
So cold here.
Alone.
Screaming into the dark.
I'm crying,
I'm praying,
My direction lost.
Rotting,
Just rotting.
Self-destructing now.

What is there for me
Now I've lost my way?
No future,
No dreams.
Embrace the darkness now.
I'm dying.
I'm losing.
Pray salvation comes.
Forgive me.
Forgive me,
When this candle fades.

All I want is freedom.
All I want is peace of mind.
All I want is an answer.
All I want is a reason to be here.
All I hear is this screaming.

All I want is to be somebody else.
All I see is this sickness.
This world is killing me.

I'm nothing.
I'm nothing.
I'm nothing but worthless dirt.

BOOK FIVE
INTERVIEWS

a pain that i'm used to

We're here to talk about your album *Self Degraded Suicide*; so first things first, why the title?
Dom Lyne: It sums up all the themes explored on the album and the emotions experienced during its creation. A lot of shit went down and I kinda beat myself up about it, put myself down and always focused on the bad, but you have to look over that and keep pushing forward.

In a way there's a feeling of hope as you follow the album through, there's always that one line at the end that proves you keep dusting yourself down and move on after every fall. It's there in each song. To be reborn you have to destroy everything you've become.

The main underlying theme of *Self Degraded Suicide* seems to be betrayal, how does that reflect to you personally?
DL: All of my lyrics are based on things I've seen, noticed or experienced, so personally they mean everything to me as they reflect what I believe. At the start, the album didn't have a theme but as it progressed it picked up the emotions of that period. There was a lot of backstabbing and deceit going on in my personal life so that kinda bled through onto the record.

Was it your way of dealing with it?
DL: [laughs] A self-flagellation therapy. No, seriously, it helped. Each song has a personal meaning, capturing the anger, upset or venom of emotion. I agree that it's not a happy album,

but it has a strong message. I mean, I wrote part of the lyrics for 'Dead in my Eyes' as I sat across from the person they were about, and then they went and stabbed me in the back and the song was completed, kinda full circle.

This loss of relationships is a theme we continued on *Judas Halo*, the follow up EP that we released shortly after.

Forgive me if I'm wrong, but is the track 'How Do You Feel Now?' referring to a guy?
DL: Yeah, you're the first person to let on that they noticed that.

It was the line 'bastard son of pain'...
DL: That's the only bit in the song that mentions the sex of the person, and if he heard it he would get the deeper meaning of the wording. But yes, it is about a dude and I'll let you draw your own conclusions to that.

The first half of the album is very political, does politics have a big say in what you do?
DL: The whole album on a whole is a critique of society, of modern culture. Everyone scrabbling for their own interests. When you talk about society you can't help but notice the increasing and distressing rise in people's apathy. They've lost sight of the bigger picture; if it doesn't affect them they don't care. The government creates all these bogeymen and dislikables through the TV sets and people just accept without question. It's very much a case of 'Saddam was a bad man, he killed loads of people, but we'll allow our government to go and kill a load of people because they haven't told us it's wrong.'

We haven't jumped on the political bandwagon; we actually have something we want to say. Today's society is shit, everyone has become disposable and we need to ask ourselves why we let it come to this.

218

So what is The Red Devil Incident up to at the moment?

DL: Well, we've just been out there promoting *Self Degraded Suicide*, performing a collection of acoustic and full band gigs. We've also been back recording some new demo tracks and new material which will form the basis of a future release.

So this isn't the last we've heard of The Red Devil Incident?

DL: [laughs] I fucking hope not, there's a lot more I wanna say and achieve.

rdi answer fan questions

August 2007

What is your inspiration as a band to make such great music? – *David Spencer*

Mark Lyne: When it comes down to inspiration, I generally take it from what I see, how I feel emotionally, and basically factors involving society, the media and basically anything that effects me as a person. That's it mainly.

Dom Lyne: Well my inspiration... most of my lyrics come post music, so obviously the lyrics I write are based upon what emotions I feel when I hear the music - the social factors, the emotional factors. When it comes down to it, it's what I hear in my head and feel when I hear the music; so emotional.

What's your favourite part about making music and what's your main goal? – *Kimi*

ML: Hearing the finished tracks because when you do them in demo they can sound a bit crap at times and you think 'oh that's bloody awful', then once you get in the studio and they're recorded as a finished product, they just sound amazing. That's the bit I love the most, when you just sit back and go 'man, that's one kickass song.'

DL: My favourite part? I hate every single bit of it. No. [laughs] No, my favourite part is hearing the final product, but because I do most of the production for it as well, to me it's about getting into the track and taking a demo that Mark's sent me, or some guitar parts he's wrote, or some lyrics I've done and taking them into the studio and moulding them into what becomes the final track that you hear. It's a long, laborious process that keeps me up for about twelve hours a day, but the end result: if [the fans are] not complaining then that makes me happy. That is actually another favourite part of mine, actually getting the feedback from the fans who say that they like the music which is the bit that makes you go 'shit, this is not shit.'

ML: And if the fans didn't like it, what's the point in making music in the first place?

DL: And the main goal, well, I'd say for me the main goal is to produce music that the fans love. It's no good if we just like it, it's for you to dance to, sing to, whatever you want to do to it... fuck to it. Also lyrically, if I was to write lyrics which move you or make you think, then if they make you feel a certain way that is the most satisfying part of the whole music making process.

Do you think the media has an impact on your music and the way your music style is? – *confused888*

DL: To a point the media has an impact, especially on the lyrics; I mean our political lyrics and our social commentaries are all based upon the media, it's putting into your mind what the media is saying and attacking it. You know the media says 'you've got to be this way' and we go 'why? Why do you have to be way, why do you have to tow a line?'

ML: Why be dictated to like herd animals?

DL: Yeah, the media does play a part in my lyric writing, but when I write my music that's all emotional, I don't sit there and go 'the world's at war I'm going to write a song,' I go 'the world's at war I'm gonna write some lyrics.' That's probably the same for you?

ML: Yeah.

What do you think the future of democracy is in the West but primarily in America and Britain who are supposed to be the so called torch bearers? – *Kevan*

DL: Well my opinion is that there isn't a democracy in England at the moment anyway. Yes we vote in a Government but that's a majority vote, it's 30% of 60% which isn't what I'd term good enough for a democracy. And the fact that we can't protest outside our own Houses of Parliament without permission from the Government that makes you think, I mean the point of a democracy is that we are allowed to have our say without permission from the people we are campaigning against. Take our current situation, we have a leader which none of us voted in as a leader, now that is not democracy, in a democracy once the leader leaves there should be a vote to see who the new leader will be and that should be down to the people because at the end of the day, the Government serves us, we don't serve them.

Who is more dangerous? These World leaders that are there for only power and money or the masses of people that follow them? – *Maja*

DL: I'd say the masses because at the end of the day, whether we like it or not, the politician is just doing their job. A politician is power, politics and money. We vote them there, we put them in that position to do that job, so if we have a problem or we don't agree, we should question them; that's the whole point of democracy, that we have a right to question our Government without fear of being attacked, put in concentration camps, being gassed or whatever.

ML: It hasn't got that far yet.

DL: Give it a few years. So yeah, in my opinion it's the masses of people who follow them because a politician is only doing what he in his brain thinks is right, and if we all follow, we're not thinking for ourselves, we're just agreeing.

Why do you think the media has such a big effect on people and why people don't think for themselves but only believe what the media serves them? – *Maja*

DL: That continues nicely from the last question because...

ML: They can't be bothered.

DL: ...the simple fact is because people can't be bothered to think for themselves, it's much easier to be told what to think, to believe what you read than it is to actually sit down and go 'you know what, I don't actually agree with that. That's actually wrong and evil.' It's just so easy to sit and do nothing, to just sit in your armchair and go 'I don't agree with that but because the media says it's right therefore it's right.' You know, you've got a mind, fucking use it.

Do any of you wear speedos? – *Dark Harvest Records*
DL: Do you wear speedos?
ML: No.
DL: No? You don't wear any underwear anyway. Do I wear speedos? No, I wear skimpy boxers that are bright green, bright red and stupid colours. Although I could be tempted to wear them if I was ever to pose. Oh, RDI photo shoot in the future. The band in speedos.
ML: You'd have to tone up like David Hasselhoff; he's the only one who's pulled off speedos.
DL: Fuck that, I'll dress like Pamela Anderson. [laughs]

between darkness and the light

Interview by Julia Cartwright
Appeared in 'Off the Wall' Fanzine – August 2007

So far 2007 seems to have been quite a good year for you. You digitally released your debut album *Self Degraded Suicide*, and have just had a solo EP released by a net-label. How have you taken that?
Dom Lyne: 2007 has been a productive year for us, like you said we released *Self Degraded Suicide* digitally, it got released earlier than the stores had told us it would and actually came out on my birthday which was, I must say, a surprise but also one of the best birthday presents you could have. Mark phoned me up and was like 'Dom, it's out. It got released today!'

Mark Lyne: It was totally by accident that I found it had come out. We'd been told it was due for an April release if it went smoothly. One morning I just went 'you know what I'll have a look' and to my surprise the album was there... my mouth hit the floor. I got on the phone to tell Dom that it was out and he was like 'What? Are you sure?' I checked again and yep the album was still there. It really made my day but more importantly it made Dom's birthday.

That must of been annoying?
DL: It really just goes to show that sometimes things don't run as smoothly as you hoped, but you just adjust to that and carry on. At the end of the day we got good feedback from it, seeing your picture in a magazine from Japan at this stage of your career is quite humbling, especially when they actually grasped

what the album was about. Also the reaction from fans was awesome and that is always the most important feedback you can receive.

When I think back about it, it has been quite a random year. I mean putting the musical releases aside we've had quite a bit of fun along the way. Getting kicked out of a venue for attacking Tony Blair's government has to be a highlight for me as it showed the power music still has.

ML: I still think the highlight of the year for me was the release of *Self Degraded Suicide* and the positive feedback, and of course, like Dom said, being asked to leave a venue just for standing up for what you believe in, that was just pathetic

We read about 'that' party on the band's web-blog. Care to elaborate?

DL: [Laughs] Ahh, *that* party. That was actually a really good night from what I remember, I was drinking wine by the pint, although I don't think I made a 'good' impression on them all. I kinda felt bad for one slight moment the next morning for them having to endure me threatening to rip people's faces off whilst I stood there wearing only vomit and my boxers.

ML: It could have been worse, you could have been naked.

DL: I was at one point, I ended up having a shower with everyone else carrying on using the toilet, so yeah, quite a few got to see me as nature intended, I even started on one guy like that. Yes, was a pretty good night. At least I made an impression.

Sounds like a bit of a rock-star moment.

DL: Well you know, we're not going to be repentant for the things we get up to when drunk, I don't believe in having regrets for what you had fun doing.

ML: Why should we feel guilty for having a good time? If people don't like it then sod them. At the end of the day it's our choice what we do and will not be told otherwise.

DL: Totally, I mean when it boils down to it, at our heart we are a tattooed rock band. We work hard; we party hard. If we want to smoke, drink and take drugs then that is up to us, and we make no apologies for that.

You've just released another digital EP through a net-label, how did that come about?
DL: Well it was a joint project really. I approached Frigida Records to see if they would be interested in releasing some of my solo works, and they said 'yes'. *Salvation Disorder No.1* doesn't represent **The Red Devil Incident** as its music stands post *Self Degraded Suicide*; it kinda shows how I experimented with sounds before we entered the studio to record it. It's the bridge gap between our original synth-less rock sound and the album. It represents a period of the band's life that I wanted to be shown.

Obviously *Salvation Disorder No.1* is literally Dom's solo works, but *Self Degraded Suicide* seems to also have that feel about it as well.
DL: Well, I did lock myself and the album away from everyone, but I wouldn't go so far as to say it was a 'solo' piece of work. It just ended up working out in a way where I'd work on it alone and only call everyone into the studio as and when they were required. I got too involved in it and as a result yeah, maybe I did lock Mark out, but at the end of the day I wouldn't change a single bit about it. It all helped create the atmosphere, and I guess almost claustrophobia, on the album.

How did that make you feel Mark, watching the album almost from the outside?
ML: At first it seemed a bit weird seeing that we tend to work together on most musical ventures, bouncing different ideas and concepts. Personally I felt that I wasn't a part of the band as Dom would not let me listen to any of the rough mixes of the songs and became very aggressive towards any suggestions I came up with, but this also helped me creatively as it fuelled

my resentment and anger. Yeah it was hard but I knew Dom had his reasons for it, and I guess as a result of all this *Self Degraded Suicide* captured the emotion of the time, it has a feeling of despair about it.

DL: With the new material we've been working on and recording, the process has been totally different. I've learnt from *Self Degraded Suicide*. Mark is involved in virtually all the studio sessions we've had, he's been there even if he's not been recording, I mean you can even hear us having conversations between vocal parts, which is always funny to listen back to. The whole atmosphere in the recording process at the moment is much more fun, more enjoyable and that is reflected in the music we're recording. It's not so dark and oppressive, there's more hope in it. I'll always see **RDI** as my baby, but like any parent knows, you have to give it space to breathe and expand, not smother it.

ML: It now feels more like a band, we have a laugh and mess about but when the red light comes on we know to be serious and get on with it. The new material is more 'upbeat', the dark songs are still there but have moved away from despair and hopelessness to hope and enlightenment.

DL: The good thing about having Mark involved more is that we're bringing back into the band more of the original elements he'd put in place. *Self Degraded Suicide* was more synth led, the guitars were supplemental almost, with our new tunes the guitars play on an equal level to the synths. **RDI** is always about evolving and improving as a band. Mark is as much of a part of the band as I am, and although he'll be the first to deny his sheer importance, **The Red Devil Incident** wouldn't be the band it is without him. Even when I was off recording *Self Degraded Suicide*, he was constantly on the other end of the phone with his support. There's some people you know you can't function without, and I know he's one of those.

You seem to be in a happier place from the last time we

met. Is that part of a new outlook?

DL: I wouldn't say that it's part of a 'new outlook'; it's more to do with the fact that we've made peace with certain parts of our lives. Obviously I'm not the same person who recorded *Self Degraded Suicide*; I mean I was a mess at that time. I don't think I let anyone really understand how far I fucked myself up, especially at the start of it all.

ML: That was difficult for me as I had no way off reaching him other than through a phone and it hurt, I can read Dom like a book and can pick up when he is in self-destruct mode but he has the annoying habit of locking away in himself and refusing to let people in. He got himself through it, and I'm sure locking himself away with the album helped, but we've both moved on since *Self Degraded Suicide*, as one door closes another opens with new problems and challenges to be faced. We are constantly evolving and reflecting on the past but not letting it get in our way or pull us down.

DL: I think last time we spoke I said in order to be reborn you have to destroy what you've become, that's really what happened. I've emerged from the flames and am more determined to get the band's message across. In a sense it's like I've saved myself, now I want to save the masses. I want people to learn from us, to grow. I mean having fans say that your music affects them is a truly beautiful moment. Even if you only change one life, that is one soul you've helped.

the devil may care

Interview by Alan Burdett
August 2008

'Don't be naughty, be good, do this, do that, be safe!' It seems the Labour party want to bring up a country of Puritans. Where have all the real rebels gone?! Especially at a time when we need them more than ever before! Why is there a lack of artists and celebrities setting an example and raising their middle fingers at this flag-less, sexless PC nation?

Dom Lyne: The simple answer would be that it's 'safe' and easier to just keep your mouth shut. Danger seems to be a bad word at the moment in this country, there's so much to rebel against but everyone is too scared to stand up. Most of the artists are placing their allegiance to all the 'stop the knives' and 'stop the ASBO youth' campaigns because it is the current trend. I'd say it's true to say most, if not all the rock rebels are in the USA and they are generally the older artists which is a shame.

There are too many restrictive laws in this country; it seems like all the freedoms and possibilities are being squeezed out of us and we're all being forced into a cattle-cage where we can simply just exist on a level that isn't detrimental to our 'beloved' dictatorship. We need to make a stand, make people open their eyes and step up. Ok, let's say something controversial, the reason there is an increase in youth disorder is not because it's something new, it has always been there, it's just reported more to make a political statement and draw people's attentions away from the real problems. The youth are rebelling for the simple reason that they are the only people who realise there is absolutely nothing in this country that is worthwhile.

I wouldn't say there is a lack of artists or celebrities, I mean look at Pete Doherty, Amy Winehouse, Kate Moss and even Naomi Campbell's recent controversy. Yeah they're old faces, but a prime example of how rebels get bad press, but bad press is good press, it means people are talking about you.

Dom, we need you to scream and punch your way onto the 'celebrity' scene as unfortunately for us that's all the masses seem to care about and listen to. This country needs some controversy, any chance of a ten in a bed sex orgy with your band mates? Will you be our next stomach pumping, smack, crack, and punk nightmare to be plastered across *Heat Magazine* and upset mums across the globe?

DL: [laughs] Sounds like a good weekend to me. Seriously though, I wouldn't share my ten in a bed orgy with anyone! Breaking into a 'celebrity' scene is quite hard unless you have big tits and blonde hair (even if they're fake). It is true that we need some pure controversy, but it depends on what level. I haven't got a problem being seen as a drunkard, drug-fuelled low-life who upsets the moral majority, but by the same token I want people to listen to what I say. It would actually be an honour to appear in *Heat* for waking up in a pool of vomit next to some starlet, mainly because so many people read the pointless crap they spit out. That is the saddest part of our society; the majority are more concerned about the lives of celebrities over the facts of war and poverty. People like to feel superior to those who have what they secretly desire, which is why everyone is so quick to put down those who have it.

***Judas Inferno* is being released by the Net-label Ekleipsi in September. Why have you done a cover of 'Chasing Cars'? It is a good cover but somehow seems out of character; did**

'a love in your life' play a part in your decision to include it on the EP and make it in the first place?

DL: We'd planned to cover it for sometime before we actually got round to doing it. When I suggested it for this EP it was agreed it was something both Mark and I needed to do at that moment. He wanted a song to dedicate to his latest 'flame' and I was affected by the lyrics - the whole question of having someone who would just be there regardless of what anyone says. Was it for a love in my life? It became that in the end, namely because I didn't want to cover the song which was suggested by my brother for my 'love', so we just gave it a joint dedication. I did feel a little hollow when I showed my boyfriend at the time and he almost cried, but it gave him something to believe in I guess.

I like the fact it seems out of character with the rest of *Judas Inferno*, you have all this anger and self-pity on the EP and then there's this 'love' song in the middle. It's like a beacon of hope that in all the mess that was going on inside my head at that time there was one person who I could rely on to be there for me, and just sit and not need anything from me. Then when you look back at the track order you can see the truth behind it all; in that context it is nothing but placing hope in someone else when you feel you have nothing. I think the track 'Lost' sums up the whole of *Judas Inferno*. I needed to be someone else instead of me and being with that person helped me be that. I think it's interesting to note that both people we dedicated the song to left our lives within weeks of each other, and both Mark and I went on to be with people who we feel truly comfortable with.

It seems fair to say that *Judas Inferno* was a solo project. What can we expect from the second album? An industrial Rock band collaboration or a synth-pop solo project?

DL: *Judas Inferno* captures a moment of my life. The emotion captured as it happened. All the anger and self-hatred you hear in the lyrics is true. Think of it as the end of a trilogy started in

Self Degraded Suicide. That's why I chose the title for it. The final burning of the phoenix in the flames before the re-birth. That whole period of my life was marred with broken relationships and a quest to find not just myself but my place in the world. Although Mark and Jorge were involved along the way, **RDI**'s releases have been pretty much solo projects, but without their support they wouldn't have come about.

Our second full-length album is definitely a collaboration of every part of the **RDI** collective. We've been working on it since late 2006, so it has definitely been a long term project for us and we've finally recorded all the parts and it's into the mixing stage. It was nice because we haven't been working to deadlines, just entering the studio when we could and just taking our time defining the album's sound. It most certainly is not a synth-pop record this time round. It's **RDI** firing on all cylinders, it's more political, more critical of society, yet still maintains the personal vulnerability that makes **RDI** what it is. **RDI** is constantly evolving and although we know what defines us at our core we're always trying to push the boundaries of what we do and not be limited into producing the same music again and again.

In my eyes it's your vocals that give RDI that addictive and moving element. It's what I and many other fans look forward to hearing most; we wait to see how you've changed and developed and what they reveal. Do you have any plans to get back into the studio and record any new vocals? To add to this question will we get to see Dom sing live in the near future?

DL: Although I wouldn't say it was just my vocals that defines **RDI**, but they certainly give us a unique sound, our marmite 'love it, hate it.' I did read once someone saying that 'it is the singer that makes this addictive like it's a drug', and it's always nice to be referred to as a drug. With each **RDI** release the vocals improve and I add new aspects to it, none more so than in the material for our second album where they have to compete with a lot of different aspects. At the moment there isn't any plans for me to get into the studio again to record, but I never rule out the possibility of it. The next vocals you'll hear will be on the album and possibly a few more covers – we've got a few of those planned.

As for the live work I love it, there isn't any plans for the next few months. I love performing live, it gives the music so much more character and variation, a different lease of life, which is why I'm glad **RDI** is so versatile, we can just walk on stage with an acoustic guitar and still be ourselves. There are plans for a live show being formulated and I just gave a hint towards what it may be. Until then my lips are sealed.

Is it still your main goal to produce music for your fans?
DL: RDI's goal is always to make music for our fans but we are not governed by that solely. Our music is for anyone. Musical integrity is always down to the band, and we will always be pushing our sound forward and not getting comfortable in one style. Hopefully our fans respect us enough to follow our journey and remain a part of the **RDI** army. We are truly grateful to all those who support us.

I like the soundtrack tracks you did for *Infection*. Granted it is a short film, what are your thoughts on it?
DL: It had its charm. We were asked to provide some music so we did, and I am not the sort of person to judge someone's ability based on one output. They made a short based upon what the resources they had. If everyone was judged on their beginnings we'd all be pretty fucked. I wish them all the best in what they do in the future.

You're in a lift, Tommy Lee, Marilyn Manson and Pamela Anderson walk in and they all ask the same question simultaneously: 'What do you want most out of life above all else?' You have twenty seconds to answer before they all depart at the next floor... No cheating! I control this lift!

DL: A threesome with Tommy and Pamela, Manson can hold the camera. No, seriously. I want to open minds and make them think differently. To be an influence on someone's life without actually physically meeting them. To connect with another soul and make them realise they are not alone, or that things can get better.

Same question, different faces. You're in a lift, God walks in and asks the question: 'What do you want most out of life above all else?' You have twenty seconds to answer before he/she/it departs at the next floor.
DL: Daddy you know this, I want your job because I'd do it so much better.

www.ingramcontent.com/pod-product-compliance
Lightning Source LLC
Chambersburg PA
CBHW031505270326
41930CB00006B/263